THE UNOFFICIAL
BATMAN TRIVIA CHALLENGE

TEST YOUR KNOWLEDGE AND PROVE YOU'RE A REAL FAN!

ALAN KISTLER,
creator and co-host of *Crazy Sexy Geeks*

This book is unofficial and unauthorized. It is not authorized, approved, licensed, or endorsed by DC Comics, Inc., Time Warner, Inc., or any of their licensees.

A adamsmedia
Avon, Massachusetts

Copyright © 2012 by F+W Media, Inc.
All rights reserved.
This book, or parts thereof, may not be reproduced in any
form without permission from the publisher; exceptions are
made for brief excerpts used in published reviews.

Published by
Adams Media, a division of F+W Media, Inc.
57 Littlefield Street, Avon, MA 02322. U.S.A.
www.adamsmedia.com

ISBN 10: 1-4405-4258-9
ISBN 13: 978-1-4405-4258-9
eISBN 10: 1-4405-4283-X
eISBN 13: 978-1-4405-4283-1

Printed in the United States of America.

10 9 8 7 6 5 4 3 2 1

Library of Congress Cataloging-in-Publication Data
is available from the publisher.

Many of the designations used by manufacturers and sellers to distinguish their product
are claimed as trademarks. Where those designations appear in this book and Adams
Media was aware of a trademark claim, the designations have been printed with initial
capital letters.

This book is available at quantity discounts for bulk purchases.
For information, please call 1-800-289-0963.

DEDICATION

To my grandparents Marie and Alan Kistler, who encouraged my first journeys into Gotham City. And to our friend Jack Burnley, an artist who did not get enough credit during his years working on Batman and other characters and who first educated me on the history and versatility of the Dark Knight.

ACKNOWLEDGMENTS

When dealing with a character whose adventures have been in continuous publication for over seven decades, it is impossible to put together a book like this without help along the way. Lisa McMullan was a constant support and reminded me to take necessary breaks before my mind became overwhelmed with jotting down Batman facts. Thanks to Robert Greenberger, a veteran of Marvel and DC Comics, as well as the author of *The Essential Batman Encyclopedia*. Kiri Callaghan was very helpful in the late hours of the night, making sure my sidebars and questions were clear. Jennifer Ewing effectively played both a support role and that of taskmaster, making sure my mind didn't wander too much in the midst of my work.

Brandi Bowles is a fine agent and effectively helped bring this project into being. Over at Adams Media, Victoria Sandbrook was a joy to work with again, and she and Peter Archer were very patient and open in their communications with me as we put this all together.

Finally, thanks to all the writers, artists, directors, producers, and storytellers who have each given life to some aspect of the Batman, creating a modern-day mythology that will outlast us all.

CONTENTS

Introduction

People the world over may recognize Batman, even by the shape of his shadow, and yet argue over who he is. It depends on how you've entered the world of the Dark Knight and how much exposure you've had to the rest of his strange multiverse.

If you began with the 1989 film *Batman*, directed by Tim Burton, you may think of Bruce Wayne as a strange, slightly awkward business-man who then becomes a dark vigilante at night, repeatedly placing his enemies in situations where they're sure to die. If you began with the live-action TV show from the 1960s that starred Adam West and Burt Ward as the dynamic duo, your first impression of Batman is not the Dark Knight but a Caped Crusader, wearing a blue and gray outfit as he openly worked as a recognized law enforcement official, chasing down criminals in broad daylight. The villains committed strange crimes but, more often than not, didn't seem interested in threatening innocent lives. A similar Batman appears in the recent cartoon series *Batman: The Brave and the Bold*, one who takes himself more seriously than the Adam West incarnation and deals with more dangerous threats, yet still engages in puns, heavy alliteration, and refers to his fists as the "hammers of justice."

And then there is the version that has stalked the comic book pages for decades, captured in film adaptations directed by Chris Nolan, and in various cartoon adventures, beginning with *Batman: The Animated*

Series in the 1990s. This Batman is a dark creature of the night, but not lethal like Burton's vision. All life is precious to him, and while he fights monsters, he refuses to live by their rules or adopt their morality. Justice is not supposed to be easy and principles cannot be abandoned when they are inconvenient. Like the other incarnations, he has no superhuman abilities—but try telling that to some of the criminals he faces. All they see is a dark winged creature with long ears that resemble devil horns, one whose eyes are blank, reflective mirrors, a being who leaps from the shadows, shrugs off gunfire, can fire blades from his hands, and then vanishes again before you even have a chance to lay a hand on him. He is truly a Dark Knight of Gotham City, traveling the world in his pursuit of criminals and evil.

Wayne is attending the theater (or, in one version, the opera) with his parents, Thomas and Martha. Both adults come from wealthy families, and both have spoken to their son of the importance of helping others less fortunate. They leave the theater and walk through an alleyway. (Depending on your version of the story, they do this out of convenience or because it's a short cut to a clinic run by a dear friend of Thomas's.) A mugger named Joe Chill lies in wait. He wants Martha's pearls and when he grows impatient and reaches for them, Thomas Wayne tries to protect his wife. Panicked, the mugger fires his first shot into Thomas, followed by another as he silences Martha's screams. As Joe Chill runs from the scene of his crime (often leaving his gun behind in the comic book stories), Bruce Wayne is left alone, kneeling in his parents' blood; his universe has just been destroyed.

In most versions of the origin, Bruce has survivor's guilt—the boy believes he could have done *something* to save his parents. In some comics, Bruce asked his mother to wear her pearl necklace that night to make the evening special as he rarely had a chance to spend time with both parents. He recalls this fact with shame after the murder, realizing the first thing the mugger asked for was the necklace. In the film *Batman Begins*, Bruce blames himself because the young boy was frightened by the show, which led to the Waynes leaving through the side door, directly into the path of a mugger. Whatever the case, a child (between eight and ten years old) believes this murder is his fault.

Bruce Wayne had every reason to become a villain. He could have allowed his guilt to corrupt him, choosing a path of self-destruction. He could have decided that his parents were wrong, that the lower classes are not worth helping if one is willing to kill two people who tried to help them. He could have concluded that the world is a bleak place without order and the only sane response is to embrace it. Instead, he chose a different path. No one else would suffer as he had. No one else would know this pain—not if he could help it.

No matter the incarnation, the story begins the same way. After years of traveling the world, gaining what knowledge he needed, training his body and mind to their peak, Bruce Wayne was ready to start his crusade in earnest. And now comes the totem.

Starting from the first revelation of his origin, comic book readers saw Bruce Wayne in his study, wondering what was still missing from his arsenal. He wanted criminals to fear him as a supernatural force rather than a mortal man, believing it was the necessary edge required to survive and quickly build a reputation. As he remarks that he must play on the fears of criminals, noting that they are a "superstitious, cowardly lot," the universe responds: a bat flies in through the window, an omen. In the 1986 retelling of the origin story, *Batman: Year One*, Bruce is suffering blood loss from a gunshot wound when this happens, and just as he rings a bell to summon Alfred's aid, a moment before he loses consciousness, he whispers, *"Yes, father . . . I shall become a bat."*

The questions in this book relate to all of Batman's various incarnations across media. There are also questions about the many alternate realities that exist within the multiverse of DC Comics. And there are questions dealing with the occasional shifts of continuity that occur in the DC Universe (or DCU). For those not familiar with these shifts, DC Comics has occasionally rebooted the majority of its fictional universe in an effort to streamline continuity, both to stay relevant with a new generation of readers and to remove/revise story elements that are now considered unnecessary, confusing, or in opposition to the new vision of certain characters.

The first version of Batman operated in the Golden Age of Comics (roughly 1935–1951) and suffered a continuity shift just a little over a year after his introduction when the stories began saying that he never used lethal force or carried a gun, despite earlier evidence to the contrary. The next major shift of Batman's canon came in 1964, several years after the Silver Age of Comics had begun. New editor Julius Schwartz decided to largely ignore the Batman stories published before that year, wanting to focus on the Caped Crusader as a serious detective and believing that the previous era had involved too much silliness. It was later said that the stories of the Golden Age Batman had actually taken place in a parallel world called Earth-2, a separate reality from the mainstream DC Universe where Batman (and others) had been born earlier and had begun operating in 1939. The modern day Batman and his colleagues were said to inhabit Earth-1, where they were in the prime of life. Eventually, the Earth-2 Batman came out of retirement for one last adventure and sacrificed his life to save Gotham City.

In 1986, a story called *Crisis on Infinite Earths* reset most of the DC Comics universe, combining various elements from Earth-1 and Earth-2 into a new, unified timeline and updating several character backstories. Batman's new past (and that of his friend Commissioner Jim Gordon) was presented in the now-famous *Batman: Year One*. Due to various factors, pieces of this "Post-Crisis" continuity contradicted each other and required constant explanation or revision. In 2011, DC reset its fictional history yet again, in an event known as the New 52; all of the DC mainstream titles ended, and fifty-two new titles emerged the next month. In this continuity, Earth-2 and its inhabitants are once again treated as a separate reality. As of 2011, the mainstream comics feature the Batman who is nearly identical to his previous incarnation, though he is a few years younger and some of his history with other superheroes has been altered. Likewise, his main allies such as Jim Gordon, the Batgirls, and the Robins are all a bit younger and less experienced now as well.

To keep things simple, I'll refer to the reboots only when necessary. Otherwise, these questions focus on the general history of the Darknight Detective who first appeared in 1939 and, amazingly, has remained in continuous publication ever since, a feat only surpassed by Superman, who appeared a year earlier. You can use these questions

to improve your geek education or as a game to wile away a lazy after-
noon, by yourself or with a friend. Perhaps one of you has read all the
tie-in novels but knows nothing of the alternate universes. Perhaps
you know the films and cartoons very well, but not the original comic
books. Whatever your background, this book will challenge you and
increase your knowledge of Gotham City's winged avenger.

And so, in the words of a certain near-immortal bat-villain . . . Are
you ready to begin?

How to Use This Book

*O*nce you've put yourself through your bat-paces, it'll be time to tally up your score. Do you have what it takes to entertain Bob Kane himself? Or are you still a newbie who needs a bit more practice?

Answer the questions in one of the quizzes, and check your answers in the key at the end of every chapter. Each answer is worth one point. That means that while most questions are just worth one point, matching questions can earn you up to 6 points if you pair the answers correctly! Tally your points and see how well you did in the chapter scorecard.

Once you've taken all nine quizzes, flip to the Fan Scorecard at the end of the book. Add your scores for each chapter and see if you're worthy of admission to the Bat-cave!

CHAPTER 1

THE DARK KNIGHT HIMSELF

*H*e was born Bruce Wayne, son of Thomas and Martha, but has gained many titles over the years. The Masked Manhunter. The Darknight Detective. The Caped Crusader. The Winged Avenger. The World's Greatest Detective. The Dark Knight. Or simply, the Batman. For over seven decades, he has entertained many with his adventures, solving a mystery or battling a fantastic menace. His basic origin is known to millions of people around the world and has been depicted across media.

Even the Batman's symbol is known around the world; he is one of the few superheroes whom you can recognize solely by his silhouette. But who is he truly and how did he come into existence? What brought this character to life? What secrets are hidden behind the demonic cowl he wears? What equipment and weaponry does he use in his dark crusade, and how has it evolved over the years? Where does he get those wonderful toys?

Just how much do you truly know about Gotham City's dark angel?

1. Although Batman made his debut in *Detective Comics* #27 (1939), he was not considered important enough to appear on the cover.

○ **A.** True

○ **B.** False

2. In his early comic book adventures, Bruce Wayne had a girlfriend who later became his fiancée. What was her name?

_____

3. Batman keeps a journal of cases involving forces he can't explain, as well as adventures that call into question his perception of reality. What does he call this journal?

_____

4. In the miniseries *The OMAC Project,* Batman created a satellite programmed to observe Earth's superhumans, both heroes and villains, and help find ways to defeat the villains. What was the original name of this satellite?

_____

5. In the 1970s, Bruce Wayne dated an actress who figured out his secret identity. He cared so much about her that (after she left because of his double life) he actually considered giving up his role as Batman. What was her name?

_____

6. As shown in *Batman: Secret Files & Origins* #1, Bruce Wayne's first nights as a crime-fighter had him wearing a plain black bodysuit and a simple ski mask as a disguise.

○ **A.** True

○ **B.** False

CLOTHES MAKE THE MAN

Batman's uniform was first truly described as body armor following the reality-changing events of the story *Crisis on Infinite Earths*. Starting in the 1990s, comics said the batsuit was constructed from a special Wayne Enterprises blend of Nomex fire-resistant material and triple-weave Kevlar. Later on, the suit was insulated against electricity, the gloves modified to be radiation proof, and an extra layer of protection was added to the neck to prevent garrote attack. And then there's the cape, which we'll discuss later.

7. During the story *Final Crisis,* the evil New God called Darkseid arranged for Batman to be captured and imprisoned. What did the villain hope to achieve?

○ **A.** Darkseid believed Batman's mind held the last key needed to reveal the Anti-Life Equation, which would let him control the minds of others.

○ **B.** Darkseid respected Batman's ability to defeat more powerful opponents and hoped to create an army of clones from him that would be nearly invincible.

○ **C.** Darkseid believed that Batman was the only man on Earth who knew Superman's mind and biology well enough to be able to kill him.

○ **D.** Darkseid knew that Batman had figured out ways to defeat most of Earth's superheroes and he wanted to extract those secrets from the Dark Knight's mind.

8. According to the Golden Age Batman stories, Bruce Wayne was majoring in what subject in college?

_____

9. Thanks to the scientist Professor Nichols, Batman and Robin once traveled back in time and met what Renaissance artist?

_____

10. The Joker was featured in Batman's first comic book adventure.

○ **A.** True

○ **B.** False

11. According to _Batman_ Vol. 1 #673, how long did Bruce Wayne train with "ninja shadow masters" in the Far East?

○ **A.** One year

○ **B.** Two years

○ **C.** Five years

○ **D.** Eight years

○ **E.** Ten years

12. When he was just a teenager, Bruce Wayne had his first hands-on training in how to track down criminals by spending time with an American private detective. In _Detective Comics Annual_ #2 (1989), the detective and a teenage Bruce Wayne ran across the Ku Klux Klan. Who was this detective?

_____

13. As revealed in the story *JLA: Tower of Babel,* Batman created his own version of the ore known as Red Kryptonite. What did this glowing red rock do to Superman?

- ○ **A.** It counteracted all effects of Green Kryptonite poisoning.

- ○ **B.** It reduced his powers so that he could only withstand ballistics weaker than the shell fired by a tank, was barely faster than a commercial train, and instead of flying he could now leap roughly one-eighth of a mile.

- ○ **C.** It caused his skin to become transparent, forcing his body to absorb so much solar radiation at once that he suffered enormous pain. This would incapacitate but not kill him.

- ○ **D.** It removed Superman's powers for twenty-four hours, allowing Clark Kent to do normal things like have a physical examination or whatever else might reveal his alien heritage under other circumstances.

14. As a child, Bruce had a friend around his age who was a frequent companion and with whom he often played chess. Who is this other boy?

_____

15. In a 1956 story that has since been removed from continuity, Batman discovered that the mugger who killed his parents had been working for a crime lord. Who was this crime lord?

- ○ **A.** Carmine Falcone

- ○ **B.** Rupert Thorne

- ○ **C.** Lew Moxon

- ○ **D.** Lionel Luthor

THOSE WONDERFUL TOYS

In the past, Bruce Wayne had to supply himself with crime-fighting tools by stealing equipment from his own company, whether it be abandoned military hardware or a new type of computer. Now that Bruce Wayne has gone public as the financial backer of the Dark Knight and Batman, Inc., he is able to directly ask Wayne Industries CEO Lucius Fox to supply the weapons needed to continue his crusade against crime.

16. In the 1940s, Bruce Wayne's love interest, Julie Madison, assumed a stage name for her acting career. What was it?

_____

17. Sasha Bordeaux and Bruce Wayne had feelings for each other and, for a brief time, Sasha operated as a masked apprentice to Batman. How did Sasha and Bruce first meet?

_____

18. In several stories, a trophy in the Batcave displays a costume similar to the Dark Knight's. Its label says it belonged to the "first" Batman. Who wore this costume?

_____

19. The person from Question 18 was not a superhero himself; nor did he attempt to become a vigilante. Why was he wearing the costume?

_____

20. According to most comics, what rereleased movie did Bruce and his parents see the night that they were murdered?

- ○ **A.** *The Scarlet Pimpernel*
- ○ **B.** *The Mark of Zorro*
- ○ **C.** *The Shadow Strikes!*
- ○ **D.** *The Count of Monte Cristo*

21. Pre-Crisis, a housekeeper helped raise young Bruce Wayne of Earth-1 after his parents were gone. What was her name?

_____

22. What color was Batman's first car? _____

23. Before he had a Batplane, what flying vehicle did the Dark Knight use, introduced in *Detective Comics* #31?

_____

ORIGIN OF THE BATMOBILE

Batman's first car was a supercharged sedan. This was followed by a dark high-performance car and then by a red sedan with a bat hood ornament. After the vehicle was labeled the "Batmobile," artist Jerry Robinson redesigned it as a black, supercharged, armored car with gadgets, batwing fins, scalloped fenders, and a bat-head battering ram. Many readers consider Robinson's design to be the definitive "original Batmobile." This car was destroyed after its debut but was replaced with a new model the very next issue, indicating Batman was constantly building new Batmobiles!

24. When Bruce used the Batplane against Professor Strange's "monster men," what major weapon did it sport, one that DC later decided made Batman seem too vicious?

○ **A.** A machine gun

○ **B.** A missile launcher

○ **C.** A flamethrower

○ **D.** A gun that shot angry bats armed with their own tiny guns

25. Concerning the housekeeper mentioned in Question 21, who was her son?

_____

26. When the evil god Darkseid sent Batman backward in time, the Dark Knight found himself in a cave. What DC character was in the cave, living out his final moments?

_____

27. In his early adventures in 1939 and the 1940s, Batman's suit was simply an acrobatic outfit with some bulletproof material guarding a large part of his front torso.

○ **A.** True

○ **B.** False

28. In the first issue of *The Return of Bruce Wayne*, the Dark Knight found himself in prehistoric times and encountered a younger version of the near-immortal villain known as Vandal Savage. In those far-off days, what was Vandal Savage called?

_____

29. When Batman first met a certain vigilante who was introduced on radio in 1930, he said that the older hero had been an inspiration to him. Who was this mysterious figure?

_____

30. When Sasha Bordeaux operated alongside Batman, what code name did she use?

○ **A.** Batgirl

○ **B.** Sparrow

○ **C.** Cover

○ **D.** She didn't use a code name, though once she referred to herself as Cover.

31. According to some accounts, Bruce Wayne initially tried to become an FBI agent before deciding to operate as a vigilante. In his FBI exams, in what area did he not receive top marks?

_____

32. Why did Bruce Wayne decide the FBI was not for him?

_____

33. According to an issue of *Starman*, what is Bruce Wayne's favorite Woody Allen film?

_____

34. Starting in childhood, Bruce began a long-distance game of chess with a pen pal whose true identity he didn't know. As adults, they continued playing against each other on a regular basis, sending moves via e-mail. Who was Bruce's unseen chess opponent?

_____

35. In the story *Infinite Crisis*, Batman became so infuriated with a villain that he drew a gun on him. Who was this villain?

_____

36. What had the villain of Question 35 done that enraged Batman so much?

○ **A.** Killed Batman's apprentice and ally, Stephanie Brown

○ **B.** Resurrected and corrupted Jason Todd

○ **C.** Injured Jim Gordon, putting him in a coma

○ **D.** The young clone hero Superboy had died while fighting the villain and Batman was enraged by the death of a young hero and by the knowledge that Superman was now suffering both grief and guilt.

37. Professor Carter Nichols helped Batman and the original Robin transfer themselves through time in various adventures. In *Batman* #700, what did the Dark Knight call the machine that Nichols used to achieve his strange form of mental projection time travel?

_____

WINGED CLOAK

The initial Batman comics showed the cape becoming rigid batwings when the Dark Knight would leap, as if they had been designed like a hang glider, helping him travel from rooftop to rooftop. Eventually, the cape lost this quality and would appear more operatic, though it would still often give the impression of a glider or parachute when Batman would leap from rooftops. In the 1990s, Batman showed that an electrical charge from his belt would cause the cape to form into rigid wings. The charge is activated via circuit-wafer controls in his gloves. Years later, the film *Batman Begins* called this feature "memory cloth."

38. By 1964, sales of Batman comics had fallen so much that, according to Bob Kane, DC Comics considered simply canceling the hero's stories or killing him off.

○ **A.** True

○ **B.** False

39. How long did Bruce stay with the Brotherhood of the Ten-Eyed Men?

_____

40. While he was training to become Batman, Bruce Wayne often used the alias Frank Dixon. This is a reference to Franklin W. Dixon, the collective pseudonym used by ghostwriters for what famous detective series?

_____

41. Evidently disagreeing with the usual standard that Bruce lost his parents when he was either eight or ten, how old did *Batman: Year One* say the boy had been?

_____

THE BAT-COLLECTION

Initially, Batman just had a couple of basic weapons. Smoke and gas bombs, a rope, and the batarang. In the 1950s and '60s, the Dark Knight seemed to be surrounded by items with a bat-prefix. As Batman became more serious again in the 1970s, many of these items went away and utility belt went back to basics. These days, since it seems unlikely that Bruce would be so whimsical as to name his equipment "batarang" or the "Batmobile," the names have been blamed on Alfred's sense of humor.

42. According to the series *Batman and the Monster Men* and *Batman and the Mad Monk*, how did Jim Gordon contact Batman before the Bat-Signal was created?

○ **A.** Gordon contacted him on a scrambled line, which would set off a special red phone in Wayne Manor.

○ **B.** Gordon got on the police radio and called for Unit 13.

○ **C.** Gordon had a special pager that would send a signal to Batman.

○ **D.** Gordon would leave a message on an encrypted website that couldn't be traced to an IP server or address.

43. According to *Batman and the Mad Monk*, why did Gordon prefer to use the Bat-Signal rather than his previous method of contacting the Dark Knight for help?

_____

44. When Bruce Wayne was interviewed on a late-night radio show, he wound up dating the host for some time. What was the name of this woman? (Hint: Her name is the Latin word for "evening.")

_____

45. In his youth, Bruce spent summer vacations playing with a young girl. Later on, she became involved in organized crime, like her father. Who is she?

_____

46. In the New 52 reboot continuity, as seen in *Justice League* #5, how old does Bruce Wayne say he was when his parents died?

_____

47. When he was researching ways to defeat the Martian Manhunter (in case the Manhunter ever went rogue), Batman figured out a way to keep these ideas and plans secret from the Martian's telepathy. What did he do?

○ **A.** He installed a telepathic guard in his cowl.

○ **B.** He programmed a posthypnotic suggestion into his own mind so he would forget about his plans until he heard a special phrase.

○ **C.** He had Robin do the research and planning and asked the young hero to keep the information secret even from him.

○ **D.** He had the sorcerer Dr. Fate install a telepathic shield over his thoughts.

48. With what actor-turned-criminal did Bruce's ex, Julie Madison, costar in one film?

_____

49. Batman's most famous cover identity is "Matches" Malone, a criminal with a North New Jersey accent. Why do people call this character "Matches"?

_____

50. In the New 52 reboot continuity it was revealed that, as a child, Bruce Wayne suspected the murder of his parents might have been more than simply a mugging. Who did he think might have ordered their deaths?

_____

51. Concerning Question 50, was young Bruce right? Was the death of Martha and Thomas Wayne more than a simple mugging?

_____

VENGEANCE AND JUSTICE

Since his origin was revealed, it's always been said that Bruce Wayne swore on his parents' graves to avenge their death by warring on all crime. But starting in the 1990s, many writers have emphasized that while Bruce may have started with vengeance in his heart, his true dedication is to prevent others from suffering as he did, losing their innocence and their loved ones to crime. He is more concerned with protection than with punishment and has often risked his own life to save hated enemies, believing that every person is worth saving and hoping that some foes may one day change.

52. One of Batman's teachers was a member of the League of Assassins who experimented with children to see if he could make them into perfect killers. What was the name of this assassin, who sometimes used a wolf as his seal?

_____

53. During the storyline *Knightquest: The Search*, Bruce Wayne traveled incognito as a British aristocrat. What alias did he use for this disguise?

- ○ **A.** Sir Hemingford Gray
- ○ **B.** Sir Darrick Gewayne
- ○ **C.** Lord William Harrison
- ○ **D.** Lord Burnley Ellsworth

54. According to a story in 1964, Bruce Wayne had an older brother named Thomas Jr. who was sent to an asylum after suffering a brain injury.

- ○ **A.** True
- ○ **B.** False

55. In the 1950s, it was said that Bruce Wayne found an activity in college to enjoy that was not directly related to his war on crime. What was this artistic pursuit?

_____

56. Pre-Crisis, it was said that Bruce Wayne was raised by a family member after the deaths of his parents. Who was this family member?

_____

57. Batman's cape has weights interwoven into the tips so he can swing it to stun opponents.

○ **A.** True

○ **B.** False

58. Why does Batman paint a large bat on his chest when it provides a target for his enemies?

_____

59. In the story line _Hush_, a criminal attempted to remove Batman's mask and was stopped by a security protocol. What happened to him?

○ **A.** He got an electric shock.

○ **B.** A small burst of gas was released from the cowl.

○ **C.** The cowl ear released pepper spray.

○ **D.** A sedative dart was fired from the buckle of Batman's utility belt.

60. What is Bruce Wayne's favorite type of tea? _____

61. Batman's cowl is equipped with a special kind of night-vision lens. What is it called?

_____

62. As seen in *Batman: The Man Who Laughs*, the Dark Knight was desperate to figure out a way to predict the Joker's state of mind. What measure did he take to accomplish this?

- ○ **A.** He had the Martian Manhunter provide a temporary telepathic link between their two minds.

- ○ **B.** Through investigation, he realized who the Joker was and interviewed the man's parents.

- ○ **C.** He found the Joker's journals and read them.

- ○ **D.** He injected himself with a small sample of the Joker's lethal venom, having realized that it drove its victims into a state of madness similar to the clown's own mind.

UPDATED BODY ARMOR

As WayneTech continued innovating new ways of miniaturizing electronics and nonlethal weapons, Batman has incorporated them into the Batsuit. After years of using the basic fire-resistant, fairly bulletproof bodysuit, Bruce got gloves that can fire projectiles, boots with retractable knives, secure broadband, a small EMP generator to disable computers or security cameras, and even a limited heating and cooling system. The battery in his belt that creates an electric charge to turn his cape into a rigid glider can also be redirected to release a 50,000-volt shock through the outer-layer of the suit, acting as a powerful taser on anyone in contact. Since this completely drains the battery, it is considered a last resort weapon.

63. What is the date of the murders of Thomas and Martha Wayne?

_____

64. During a confrontation in the sewers, Batman was technically killed. It was only thanks to the intervention of the criminal Electrocutioner that he was able to be revived.

○ **A.** True

○ **B.** False

65. Shortly before Harvey Dent became the villain Two-Face, Batman considered telling the man his own secret identity.

○ **A.** True

○ **B.** False

66. According to some comics, Bruce Wayne was born in the spring on what day?

_____

67. In 2008, the 1958 story of the Batman of Zur En Arrh was revised. Now Batman's visit to a planet called Zur En Arrh where he meets a counterpart in a similar costume is said to be a hallucination suffered as a side effect of exposure to a mind-altering chemical weapon. Whose weapon created this hallucination?

_____

68. In _Justice League_ #1 (2011), Batman admits that there is a super-hero whom he hasn't met yet but has already studied, just in case they ever came into conflict. Which superhero is he talking about?

_____

69. According to stories written by Jeph Loeb, what book did Martha Wayne read to young Bruce Wayne on rainy days?

_____

70. In the Golden Age, Batman was eventually recognized as having some authority with the Gotham City Police Department and was occasionally asked to perform missions for the government.

○ **A.** True

○ **B.** False

71. In their first comic book team-up story, Bruce Wayne and Clark Kent met under what circumstances?

○ **A.** Clark was covering a competition between Wayne Enterprises and LexCorp.

○ **B.** Clark and Bruce were on a cruise ship and forced to share a room.

○ **C.** They met when the villain Starro the Conqueror was attempting to invade Earth.

○ **D.** Bruce was staying in Metropolis for a few weeks and began dating Clark's colleague, Lois Lane.

72. What was the true name of the alien scientist who operated as the Batman of the planet Zur En Arrh?

_____

73. Like the movies directed by Chris Nolan, the comics have shown that the first Bat-Signal was actually projected by a spotlight to which Batman had tied a criminal.

○ **A.** True

○ **B.** False

74. In pre-Crisis continuity, "Matches" Malone was originally an actual criminal whom Batman had encountered. It was only after his death that Batman began disguising himself as the criminal.

○ **A.** True

○ **B.** False

NONLETHAL AVENGER

Although he occasionally used a gun in his early published stories, DC later decided to make Batman stand out from previous vigilantes such as the Shadow and the Spider by vowing to never take a life. As far as continuity is concerned, he has always operated by this code and has never officially considered guns as part of his arsenal. Batman's even saved the lives of several enemies—for example, when he prevented the Joker from being executed for a crime he hadn't committed. Despite this, there have been a few rare instances where the Dark Knight has decided not to help a villain who has proven skillful in being able to save himself from such situations. In *Batman: A Death in the Family*, the Dark Knight left the Joker, who was suffering from gunshot wounds, inside a helicopter that was about to crash in New York's East River. Moments later, the hero admitted that he had no doubt the Joker survived the incident and had already escaped. And though Batman doesn't like firearms, he has occasionally handled them in nonlethal ways, such as when he used the assassin Deathstroke's rifle to shoot a pair of guns out of the hands of a killer who was too far away for a batarang.

75. According to the story "Joe Chill in Hell," published in *Batman* #673 (2008), what was the reason Joe Chill decided not to kill young Bruce Wayne even though the boy was the only living witness to the murders of Thomas and Martha Wayne?

○ **A.** Bruce's eyes were so full of hatred, it frightened him.

○ **B.** Bruce reminded Chill of the son he'd lost.

○ **C.** Chill heard someone approaching and panicked, deciding to run rather than kill anyone else.

○ **D.** Chill has a rule against shooting children and pregnant women.

76. At one point, Batman engaged in the Thogal Ritual as part of a journey to reconnect with his original ideals and purpose. In what comic book series was the Thogal Ritual first shown?

_____

77. In the story arc *JLA: New World Order*, Batman was able to single-handedly take out multiple superpowered aliens who had already defeated and captured Green Lantern, the Flash, Aquaman, Wonder Woman, and (through trickery) Superman. What weakness had Batman discovered in his enemies?

_____

78. What does the White Martian race call Batman?

○ **A.** The Dark One

○ **B.** The Hated One

○ **C.** The Detective

○ **D.** The Knight

79. Bruce Wayne dated Pamela Isley for several weeks before encountering her as Poison Ivy.

○ **A.** True

○ **B.** False

80. According to *Batman: Dark Victory*, when did Bruce Wayne first meet gangster Carmine Falcone?

_____

81. The Thogal Ritual involved Bruce being trapped in a cave, without light or sound, for forty-nine days. What experience was this meant to simulate?

_____

82. Just in case he encounters superhumans with heightened senses, Batman lined his cowl with lead (to block X-ray vision) and created a device to mask the sound of his heartbeat.

○ **A.** True

○ **B.** False

83. After the ritual in the cave, mentioned in Question 81, Batman decided to create a backup personality in his mind, an alternate persona who would take over if his mind became completely dominated by the will of another or if he suffered a complete psychological breakdown. What was the inspiration for this programmed identity?

_____

WINDOWS TO THE SOUL

Batman was one of the first heroes to be drawn with blank, white eyes when he donned his mask. Initially, this was seen as simple artistic license. But many years later, characters in the story mentioned how they couldn't see Batman's eyes and it was revealed that the cowl had blank lenses built in, disguising the shape and color of Bruce Wayne's eyes and helping his intimidation factor. Following this, many DC heroes have used the same explanation concerning their own masks.

84. In post-Crisis continuity, Julie Madison was seen dating Bruce in what miniseries by Matt Wagner?

_____

85. After Batman's back was broken by the criminal Bane, Alfred needed to explain Bruce Wayne's very noticeable injuries and disability. What was the cover story?

- ○ **A.** Bruce had been playing polo and was thrown from his horse, falling down a steep hill.
- ○ **B.** Bruce had been skiing when an avalanche had forced him off a cliff.
- ○ **C.** While rock climbing Bruce hadn't properly secured his harness.
- ○ **D.** Bruce had accidentally driven one of his sports cars off the road.

86. On the anniversary of the death of his parents, what does Bruce Wayne do when he visits the spot where they died?

_____

87. In the miniseries mentioned in Question 84, what profession did Julie Madison hold when she met Bruce?

- ○ **A.** She was a waitress who was studying acting.
- ○ **B.** She was a law student.
- ○ **C.** She was a lounge singer.
- ○ **D.** She was a professional actress.

88. For some time, Batman had a ring with a Kryptonite stone. Who was the original owner of this ring?

_____

89. In *Detective Comics* #308 (1962), the story entitled "The Flame-Master" featured a criminal named Pete Dale using mystical relics to gain fantastic power. Batman then turned the tables on him by using the relics himself. What kind of power did these items give Batman?

_____

90. What strange story, later referenced in *Batman: R.I.P.*, was the first to feature a Batman costume with a yellow symbol?

_____

91. For a while, Batman's comic book stories featured Bruce Wayne and Dick Grayson living with a woman they called Aunt Harriet. Whose aunt was she?

_____

92. When he announced the formation of Batman, Inc., to the press, how did Bruce Wayne explain his association with the Dark Knight?

   A. He said that Batman had recently saved his life and that he wanted to return the favor by supporting his crusade against crime.

   B. He said that he had secretly been funding Batman's activities and providing him with resources for years and had now decided to be open about it.

   C. He said that this was a way of thanking Batman for recently saving all of Gotham City once again from the Joker.

   D. He said the decision had been made by his CEO, Lucius Fox, and he trusted that Lucius knew what he was doing.

93. In post-Crisis continuity, it was revealed that young Bruce Wayne lived with a relative for two years after the deaths of his parents but that he then left that home when he found out the relative was a criminal.

   ○ **A.** True

   ○ **B.** False

94. In one strange 1950s adventure, Batman got into legal trouble when it was discovered that a circus performer had been using the Batman name and a similar costume for years before Bruce ever began his war on crime.

   ○ **A.** True

   ○ **B.** False

TECHNO-BATMAN

A few times, Batman has employed specialty versions of the Batsuit for unusual situations. One is outfitted for space, another for deep-sea diving. When he needed to confront criminals in a snow-covered environment, he used a suit designed to provide camouflage against different surroundings. In *Batman vs. Predator*, he used techno-armor that better protected him from the alien killer's weapons and allowed him to see through his enemy's invisibility cloak.

95. In *Batman* #0, it was revealed that WayneTech had originally designed the first Batmobile as an armored vehicle to be used by whom?

_____

96. According to a story by Jeph Loeb and Tim Sale, Bruce Wayne and Lucius Fox first met in another city, when Bruce saved the man from muggers. Which city was this?

_____

97. In the 1950s, Batman occasionally worked with a dog named Ace. To protect the dog's identity, Batman gave Ace a mask and referred to him by what name?

_____

98. What trick concerning handwriting does Batman use to emphasize the ruse that Bruce Wayne and the Dark Knight are different people?

_____

99. The dog Ace from Question 97 wore a mask to hide a distinguishing mark on his forehead. What is the shape of this mark?

_____

100. Who was Ace's original owner in pre-Crisis continuity?

_____

101. Ace later appeared again in post-Crisis continuity as a dog belonging to a Native American. What was this man's name?

_____

102. Like his pre-Crisis counterpart, the version of Ace from Question 101 had a distinguishing mark. What was it?

_____

103. For a while, when Bruce Wayne was physically unable to act as Batman, he turned the mantle over to a warrior named Azrael, the latest in a long line of people who had used that name. What was Azrael's true name?

_____

104. When Azrael served as Batman, by what nickname did readers call him?

_____

105. Dick Grayson was Bruce Wayne's ward, meaning Bruce was his legal guardian. Bruce never officially adopted Dick Grayson as his son.

○ **A.** True

○ **B.** False

106. In addition to programming himself with an alternate personality to take over if he suffers a mental breakdown, Bruce Wayne has also hypnotized himself into forgetting he's Batman if he needs to convince people who have deduced his secret identity and intend to force him into exposing it.

○ **A.** True

○ **B.** False

STEALTH, SKILL, SMARTS

Though he has special suits of armor and access to a number of things that could make him effectively superpowered, Batman is not Iron Man. As far as Bruce Wayne is concerned, relying on techno-armor sets you up for failure, because either you forget to focus on intelligence and strategy or you'll eventually face an enemy with superior force anyway, turning your armor into dead weight. What's more, Batman relies on stealth and theatrics to give the impression that he is more than human; heavy, clunky armor tends to hinder that.

107. In a 1999 graphic novel written by Chuck Dixon, Batman was entrusted with what religious artifact?

108. Referring to the object from Question 107, to whom did Batman give the object after realizing that some of his enemies knew he had it?

_____

109. The terrorist cult leader Ra's al Ghul wanted the object from Question 107. What did he intend to do with it?

_____

110. According to _Batman_ Vol. 1 #673, Batman stalked Joe Chill during the early days of his career. What was the result of this psychological torture?

○ **A.** Joe Chill told the Joker his realization that he had created Batman by murdering the hero's parents, and the Joker responded by killing him.

○ **B.** Joe Chill was so terrified that he got drunk and deliberately walked into traffic rather than face Batman again.

○ **C.** Joe Chill committed suicide, using the same gun that he'd used to kill Thomas and Martha Wayne.

○ **D.** Joe Chill turned himself in to the police, preferring to serve time in prison rather than fear that Batman lurked in every shadow he saw.

111. According to some accounts, an ancestor of Batman's had been a knight during the Crusades who wore a bat as his crest.

○ **A.** True

○ **B.** False

112. In a pre-Crisis story, Batman was asked to become Earth's official Green Lantern. But he refused, as he did not want to divide his time between defending Gotham and the obligations he would have to the Green Lantern Corps.

○ **A.** True

○ **B.** False

113. In a 1950s story, Batman volunteered to be in a military sensory deprivation and isolation experiment for several days. What did the military hope would be the benefit of this experiment?

_____

114. As revealed in *Batman* Vol. 1 #673, what was Batman's true reason for volunteering for the isolation experiment of Question 113?

_____

115. Before becoming Batman, Jean-Paul Valley was chosen to be a warrior for what secret organization?

_____

116. Talia al Ghul gave Batman a mystical suit of armor that enhanced his abilities. What is the name of this armor?

_____

117. What is the curse of the armor mentioned in Question 116?

_____

118. Batman decided not to continue wearing the armor from Question 116. Who currently has it?

○ **A.** Dick Grayson, Nightwing

○ **B.** Michael Washington Lane, the current Azrael

○ **C.** Clark Kent, Superman, who keeps it hidden in his Fortress of Solitude

○ **D.** Diana of Themyscira, Wonder Woman, who buried it in a cave

119. The Azrael who temporarily stood in as Batman was given hypnotic programming to make him a formidable warrior. What was the name for this programming?

_____

120. When the old Azrael was acting as Batman, a few folks such as Catwoman, Bane, and Commissioner Gordon realized there was a new person behind the mask. What famous villain also realized this was a new Dark Knight, based on his fighting style?

_____

INSPIRATIONS

Starting in 1986, the post-Crisis DCU history had Batman exist in the same reality as Alan Scott, the Golden Age Green Lantern and another Gotham City hero. It was said that Scott's career was one of Bruce Wayne's biggest inspirations when he was a child and so, in a way, the Dark Knight had become a successor to the Emerald Knight. Twenty-five years later, the New 52 reality that began in 2011 once again placed Alan Scott and the modern-day Batman in separate, parallel universes, returning Bruce to his role as Gotham City's first superhero.

121. Bane broke Bruce Wayne's back, leaving him nearly dead and forcing the mantle of the Bat to pass to another. Months later, Bruce was able to walk without assistance again and retrained to return to his crusade. How did he overcome his injury?

○ **A.** He used the Lazarus Pits of Ra's al Ghul to restore his body.

○ **B.** His spine was broken but the nerves were intact. A mutant with healing abilities later restored his body.

○ **C.** He took part in an experimental surgery using nannites to rebuild the damaged areas of his spine.

○ **D.** He used Bane's own strength-enhancing drugs to boost his body's recovery abilities, painfully regenerating his spine in the process.

122. When Batman was defeated by Bane, he asked Azrael to take up the mask rather than Dick Grayson. What reason for this did he initially give Tim Drake, the third Robin?

_____

123. In *Detective Comics* #275, a strange accident left Batman's costume with zebra stripes, turning him into the "Zebra Batman" (because being named after one animal sometimes isn't enough). What superpower did he have during this temporary transformation?

_____

124. Though he did not believe in killing, Bruce Wayne willingly trained under killers and assassins, some of whom worked for Ra's al Ghul.

○ **A.** True

○ **B.** False

125. In the story arc *War Games*, readers discovered that Batman had planned a scenario that would create a power vacuum in Gotham's criminal underworld. Whom did Batman intend to step in, uniting all the crime families under his leadership?

_____

126. Along with "Matches" Malone, Batman sometimes uses the cover identity of a criminal with one hand. What is the name of this cover identity?

_____

127. Batman has occasionally disguised himself as a cop named Detective Hawke. During what storyline did Commissioner Gordon meet Detective Hawke and realize his true nature?

_____

128. Originally, it was said that Martha Wayne and Thomas Wayne were both shot by Joe Chill. This was established again post-Crisis. But for several years, several comics said that Thomas Wayne was shot and that Martha Wayne died from a different occurrence. What was it?

_____

129. As seen in *Batman: Year One*, to help give the impression that he was a supernatural creature, Bruce learned how to imitate the growl of what kind of animal?

_____

130. In post-Crisis continuity, as revealed in *Batman and the Monster Men*, the original Batmobile was an armored vehicle with no decorative elements to it. Who made a joke about the vehicle needing batwing fins, which Batman then decided was a good idea?

_____

131. Similar to the car depicted in *Batman Forever*, the Batmobile is able to scale walls due to anti-gravity units of Nth metal, technology from the planet Thanagar.

○ **A.** True

○ **B.** False

132. In *Batman* Vol. 1 #673, writer Grant Morrison combined the two different accounts of Martha Wayne's death. In his account, how exactly did she die?

_____

THE BATARANG

The batarang is Batman's most famous weapon, as closely linked to him as the Batmobile and his winged cape. Originally, it was a blunt object that operated as a boomerang. Later on, it was also often seen attached to his swing lines, helping to secure them on roof ledges and gargoyles. In the 1970s, Batman started using two versions, a blunt version meant to knock people out, and a wing-shaped throwing blade. These days, Batman's swing line is fired from an air-pressure gun and the batarangs are almost exclusively depicted as small bat-shaped blades, similar to shuriken.

133. Batman uses a grapple gun that fires a modified form of commando unit climbing gear, with high-test de-cel lines and "smart" acceleration motoring within the dart that help it dig into metal and concrete surfaces, and an industrial retracting motor. This grapple gun (or line gun) has its own fun nickname, in the same vein as Batman's batarang. What is it?

_____

134. In Mark Waid's story *JLA: Tower of Babel*, which international villain used weapons of Batman's own design to disable the Justice League?

_____

135. The Bat-signal is a well-known sight against Gotham's cloudy night sky. But on nights when the sky is clear, where is the signal aimed?

_____

136. What is Bruce Wayne's favorite soup?

_____

137. An alternate Bat-signal was once used by then Police Commissioner Michael Akins. Unlike the traditional signal, it was not a modified klieg searchlight. How did it work?

_____

138. What major company created the alternate signal of Question 137?

_____

139. Although the mayor's office and Gotham's detectives know that the Bat-signal is used to summon the Dark Knight, the GCPD does not like admitting to the public that they occasionally ask a vigilante for help. How does Commissioner Gordon explain to journalists why he occasionally shines a bat symbol into the sky?

_____

140. Along with the red phone in the Batcave, there is another "batphone" that is actually an encrypted cell phone with a built-in tracking device. Who has been seen carrying this device?

_____

141. Batman set up a personal teleport booth in the Batcave to allow instantaneous transport to the Justice League Watchtower. From what company did Batman steal the designs for such a device?

_____

142. The creation of Aunt Harriet Cooper and her moving into Wayne Manor was done in part to help reduce accusations that Batman and Robin were engaged in a gay relationship.

○ **A.** True

○ **B.** False

CALLING FOR BACKUP

Batman may be a loner by nature but he understands that sometimes you need friends. His cowl communicator can instantly make contact with Nightwing, Robin, Alfred, and others. The Justice League signal device in his belt can alert the team that he's in trouble. A hypersonic signal device hidden in his boot can also be used to summon the bats from the Batcave or, with some adjustment, a certain colorfully clad Kryptonian.

143. In one of his more bizarre stories, published in 1957 and entitled "The Rainbow Batman," the Dark Knight wore different-colored versions of his costume on different nights. Why?

_____

144. During times when he's had to unmask, Batman has had makeup and thin layers of fake skin attached to his face so that people who see him will think that he's actually someone else disguised as Bruce Wayne, his true face still hidden.

○ **A.** True

○ **B.** False

145. In the fiftieth-anniversary issue of _Detective Comics_, published in 1987, Batman met a detective whom he was surprised was still alive. Who was this person?

_____

Chapter 1 Answer Key

1. True.
2. Julie Madison.
3. The Black Casebook.
4. Brother Mark I (Brother I is an acceptable answer).
5. Silver St. Cloud.
6. True.
7. B.
8. Criminology.
9. Leonardo da Vinci.
10. False.
11. B.
12. Harvey Harris.
13. C.
14. Tommy Elliot.
15. C.
16. Portia Storme.
17. She was hired as his bodyguard.
18. Thomas Wayne.
19. He was attending a costume party and the theme was flying animals.
20. B.
21. Mrs. Chilton.
22. Red.
23. The Bat-Gyro.
24. A.
25. Joe Chill.
26. Anthro.
27. True.
28. Vandar Arg of the Blood Clan (simply saying "Vandar Arg" is fine).
29. The Shadow.
30. D.
31. Marksmanship.
32. He believed that it was hampered from fighting crime more effectively due to the paperwork, politics, and rules.
33. *Crimes and Misdemeanors.*
34. Oswald Cobblepot, the Penguin.
35. Alexander Luthor of Earth-3.
36. D.
37. The Maybe Machine.
38. True.
39. Six months.
40. The Hardy Boys.
41. Six years old.
42. C.
43. He wanted to be open to his superiors about when he was contacting Batman for help, even if it angered them.
44. Vesper Fairchild.
45. Mallory Moxon.
46. Ten years old.
47. B.
48. Basil Karlo, Clayface I.
49. He almost always has a match in his mouth.
50. The Society of Owls.
51. No.
52. David Cain.
53. A.
54. True.
55. Stage acting.
56. Uncle Philip Wayne.
57. True.
58. Because it draws enemy fire to his chest, which has thick, reinforced armor, as opposed to his head.
59. B.
60. Lapsang Suchong.
61. Starlite.
62. D.
63. June 26.
64. True.
65. True.
66. April 7.
67. Professor Milo.
68. Superman.
69. *Alice's Adventures in Wonderland.*
70. True.
71. B.
72. Tlano (pronounced "tay-lahn-oh").
73. False.
74. True.
75. B.
76. *52.*

77. They were afraid of fire, which also caused them to lose their powers.

78. B.

79. False.

80. At his parents' funeral.

81. Death.

82. True.

83. His hallucination about meeting another Batman on a planet called Zur En Arrh.

84. *Batman and the Monster Men.*

85. D.

86. He places roses on the spot where they fell, using either two long-stem roses or a wreath.

87. B.

88. Lex Luthor.

89. He commanded the four elements of fire, water, earth, and air.

90. "Batman—The Superman of Planet X!" (although "The Batman of Zur En Arrh" is an acceptable answer).

91. Dick Grayson's.

92. B.

93. False.

94. True.

95. Police SWAT teams.

96. Paris.

97. The Bat-Hound.

98. Batman is left-handed, Bruce Wayne is right-handed.

99. A star.

100. Jim Wilker.

101. Black Wolf.

102. A bat-shaped dark patch of fur.

103. Jean-Paul Valley.

104. Azbat.

105. False. Sometime after Dick Grayson had become Nightwing, Bruce offered to officially adopt him and name the young hero as his heir; Dick accepted.

106. True. This was revealed in a battle against Prof. Hugo Strange in the pages of *Batman: Gotham Knights.*

107. The Holy Grail, as seen in *Batman: The Chalice.*

108. Superman.

109. He wanted to make his daughter, Talia, immortal.

110. C.

111. True.

112. False.

113. It was to learn more about the kind of stress space travel can inflict on a person.

114. He hoped the experience would help him gain further insight into the Joker's mind.

115. The Order of St. Dumas.

116. The Suit of Sorrows.

117. It will destroy anyone who wears it who is not pure of heart by driving him or her insane.

118. B.

119. The System.

120. The Joker.

121. B.

122. As Nightwing, Dick Grayson wanted to be his own man, outside of Bruce's shadow, and Bruce said that he wanted to respect that.

123. He had power over magnetic forces, just like the villain Zebra Main, but couldn't control his ability.

124. True.

125. "Matches" Malone.

126. Lefty Knox.

127. *Cataclysm.*

128. She had a weak heart and the shock of Thomas's death caused a heart attack that killed her.

129. A leopard.

130. Alfred.

131. False.

132. Joe Chill shot her, too, but she would have survived if the ambulance had arrived in time and she hadn't had a weak heart.

133. The bat-cable or bat-line.

134. Ra's al Ghul.

135. Gordon aims the signal at a nearby skyscraper, ensuring it can still be seen for miles.

136. Mulligatawny.

137. It used a green laser to paint the signal on a cloud.

138. Kord Industries.

139. Rather than say he's signaling Batman for help, Gordon has said the signal is a scare tactic against criminals, warning them that if the cops don't catch them, Batman is still out there.

140. Commissioner Gordon.

141. S.T.A.R. Labs.

142. False.

143. Robin suffered a broken arm and Batman was trying to distract people from noticing his injury and possibly linking it to the recently injured Dick Grayson.

144. True.

145. Sherlock Holmes.

Score Your Bat-Knowledge!

In this section, there are 145 possible right answers.

If you got 0–73 right, you've got a lot of learning to do. You may have read a comic or two, but you've got a lot to learn about the Batman.

If you got 74–114 right, you're definitely a detective in the making, but hit the books a little harder before you start saying you're an expert.

If you got 115–145 right, congratulations! You know the Batman almost as well as he knows himself. Find a cape and wear it with pride, you've earned it!

CHAPTER 2

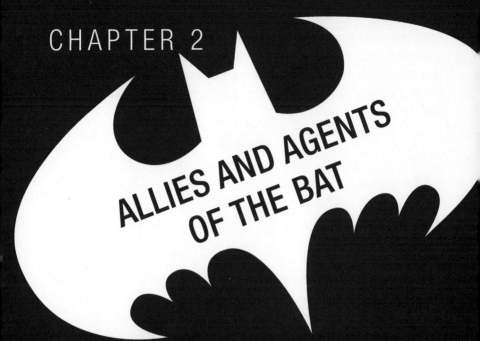

ALLIES AND AGENTS OF THE BAT

*P*eople often consider Batman the lone Dark Knight of Gotham City, the winged avenger who operates with only the aid of an honorable policeman and a military agent-turned-butler. But the fact is, Batman has operated with many allies almost since his very beginning. It was just a year after his first appearance that Batman took on his first apprentice, Dick Grayson. Since then, there have been several who have assumed the role of Robin, acting as squires to the Dark Knight. What's more, Superman and Batman have joined forces so often that they are considered the World's Finest Team. And that's not even taking into account the different superhero teams that Batman has worked with and founded. In fact, he was a founding member of DC's premier superhero strike force, the Justice League.

Despite his lack of superpowers, Batman stands on equal footing with men and women who can lift fire engines, propel themselves through force of will, summon arcane forces, and bring destruction with their very gaze. The presence of these super-powered warriors does not diminish Batman. Instead, it makes him seem all the more impressive; he can hold his own alongside them and, in some cases, outshine them. More than a few superheroes have found themselves intimidated by the blank-eyed stare of the Dark Knight.

See if you truly know the friends and comrades of the world's greatest detective!

1. In the New 52 continuity, Batman's first meeting with another genuine superhero occurs in *Justice League* #1 (2011). Who is this hero?

_____

2. When Alfred first appeared in the 1950s, his last name was said to be Beagle. Later this was said to be a stage name he had used as an actor. What, then, is his real last name?

    A. Chill

    B. Giles

    C. Grayson

    D. Pennyworth

3. At times, Alfred has seemed to have a romantic interest in what other person in Bruce Wayne's life?

_____

4. As far as official continuity is concerned, who was the first person known as Batgirl?

    ○ **A.** Betty Kane

    ○ **B.** Bette Kane

    ○ **C.** Barbara Gordon

    ○ **D.** Vicki Vale

LONGTIME ALLIES

There is a misconception that Batman was a loner for years and that the comic jumped the shark by introducing Robin as a young, immature sidekick. The historical truth is that the Dark Knight was in existence just over one year before Robin showed up. Dick Grayson was created for Batman's universe before Alfred, the Joker, Catwoman, or even the Batcave.

5. Where did Dick Grayson grow up?

○ **A.** Hill Valley

○ **B.** Gotham City

○ **C.** Metropolis

○ **D.** Haley's Circus

6. Dick Grayson lost his family when . . .

○ **A.** Two-Face killed his parents and brother with a bomb.

○ **B.** Killer Croc killed his parents for witnessing a crime.

○ **C.** Mobster Tony Zucco had his parents killed to scare their employer into cooperating.

○ **D.** Mobster Carmine Falcone had them killed due to money they owed him.

7. As a wedding gift, Batman bought an apartment for which superhero?

_____

8. Batman has worked alongside a strange hero whom many would call insane and who resembles one of his greatest enemies. Who is this person?

_____

9. Bruce had a childhood friendship with what future superhero?

○ **A.** Aquaman

○ **B.** Green Arrow

○ **C.** Zatanna

○ **D.** Black Canary

10. Batman trained under the father of the hero from Question 9. Who is this famous father?

_____

11. In London, two vigilantes model themselves after Batman and Robin. What do they call themselves?

_____

12. In the 1950s, a young Bruce Wayne visited Smallville and teamed up with a young Clark Kent. During this adventure, Bruce adopted a costumed identity. What was his furry alias in this story?

_____

13. In official DC Comics continuity (so no "possible future" or "parallel universe" stories), how many young heroes have assumed the name and costume of Robin and worked alongside Batman?

- ○ **A.** 3
- ○ **B.** 5
- ○ **C.** 4
- ○ **D.** 2

14. The second Batwoman, Kate Kane, had a military career ahead of her but was forced to leave. Why?

_____

15. What is the name of the Parisian vigilante whom Batman recruited for Batman, Inc.?

_____

16. In some comics that took place before the Crisis reboot of the 1980s, it was said that Bruce Wayne had been the first person to use the Robin identity, back when he was a teenager and a sidekick to a great detective.

- ○ **A.** True
- ○ **B.** False

17. Although he was Batman's apprentice, Dick Grayson formed his own team of teen heroes and became their leader. This team was called what?

_____

RED LEATHER THRILL-SEEKER

Robin was the first true superhero sidekick, conceived of by Bill Finger as a way of giving readers a character who seemed more like them. They may have dreamed of being Batman, but they were probably closer in personality to Robin, who looked at Bruce's bleak world and could grimace as he pointed out the absurd. While Bruce was grim and somber, Robin was a laughing daredevil, disappointed if he were surrounded only by three criminals instead of five, thrilled by the action as much as he was motivated by altruism. His bright colors announced his presence and made him a target, and he was just fine with that if it meant the night wouldn't be boring.

18. Who were the other two founding members of the team mentioned in Question 17?

_____

19. The second version of Batwoman is Kate Kane. The original Batwoman was introduced in 1956. Her real name was . . .

○ **A.** Beth Kane

○ **B.** Kathy Kane

○ **C.** Kathy DuCain

○ **D.** Roberta Kane

20. The original Batwoman was created by DC Comics to provide a noncriminal love interest for Batman, combating accusations that he and Robin were a gay couple.

○ **A.** True

○ **B.** False

21. Which of Batman's allies also operates as a police detective in Middleton, Colorado?

_____

22. Batman met Jason Todd, the second Robin, when the boy was stealing something. What was it?

_____

23. Stephanie Brown is a Gotham City superhero who has used what heroic alias?

  ○ **A.** Robin

  ○ **B.** The Spoiler

  ○ **C.** Batgirl

  ○ **D.** All of the above.

24. Which of Batman's Justice League teammates works as a crime scene investigator in his secret identity?

_____

25. What member of the Justice Society of America also called Gotham City his home?

_____

26. In 1959, Batman encountered the Bat-Mite. What was he?

  ○ **A.** A magical elf who considered himself Batman's biggest fan.

  ○ **B.** A seventh-dimensional being that resembled a cartoonish bat.

  ○ **C.** A local comic book nerd who hoped to become Batman's new sidekick.

  ○ **D.** An imperfect clone of Batman.

27. A few times, Batman and Superman have used what seems to be a special code so they can communicate secretly when they know they might be overheard by enemies. This special code is actually what language?

_____

28. During a crossover between Marvel and DC Comics, Batman met a superhero whom he quickly deduced was hiding a disability. Who was this hero?

_____

29. When Robin was being created in 1940, a few alternate names for the character were tossed around. Which of these was *not* a suggested name for Batman's apprentice?

○ **A.** Tiger

○ **B.** Wildcat

○ **C.** Socko

○ **D.** Sparrow

DIFFERENT PERSPECTIVES

Robin and Batman don't really look as if they were cut from the same cloth. Even when Robin's suit has been updated and more black has been incorporated, he is still a colorful character compared to the dark caped crusader who mentors him. Part of this is that comics as a visual medium focus on how a costume reflects a character's nature and personality. It's been explained that the costume is based on Dick Grayson's acrobat uniform and colors, connecting him with his roots. Batman has also said he allowed Robin to wear such a uniform because it lets criminals see him as the "good cop" of the duo, which has its advantages.

30. A Sioux warrior modeled himself after Batman. What did he call himself?

_____

31. Concerning the hero from Question 30, what was the heroic alias of his son and sidekick?

_____

32. During the 1980s, Batman was fed up with the Justice League, hampered as it was by diplomatic concerns with other governments. Believing that justice was more important than law or politics, Batman left and formed his own team called . . .

  ◯ **A.** The Gotham Knights

  ◯ **B.** Shadow-Force

  ◯ **C.** The Outsiders

  ◯ **D.** Batman's Action Directive Assault Super Squad

33. Batman has Alfred act as his support, often communicating with him via radio. Who acts as support via radio to the second Batwoman?

_____

34. Before becoming an actor and then the Wayne family butler, Alfred worked as a government intelligence agent.

  ◯ **A.** True

  ◯ **B.** False

35. For a time, it was said that one of Batman's teachers had been a costumed hero during the 1940s and a member of the Justice Society of America. Which superhero was this?

- ○ **A.** The Green Lantern called Alan Scott
- ○ **B.** The Sandman
- ○ **C.** Wildcat
- ○ **D.** The Shadow

36. At what famous Gotham City location did Batman first meet the second Robin?

---

37. As readers saw in *Batman: Year One*, James W. Gordon transferred to Gotham City PD after leaving what major city?

- ○ **A.** Metropolis
- ○ **B.** New York City
- ○ **C.** Washington, D.C.
- ○ **D.** Chicago

THE WORLD'S FINEST TEAM

World's Finest Comics began as a ninety-six-page quarterly anthology in 1941. Nearly every issue featured Batman and Superman, though the two never actually met in the comics until 1954. Since then, the two have been nicknamed the *World's Finest Team*. Polar opposites, they have proven an entertaining and formidable force, each complementing the other's strengths. At times, their opposite natures have made for excellent drama. When DC Comics rebooted history in 1986, Superman and Batman didn't fully trust each other. Slowly they grew into respected colleagues and then evolved into brothers-in-arms, each ready to die for the other.

38. An ally of Batman operates in the Congo. His real name is David Zavimbe. What is the name of his costumed identity?

---

39. The daughter of one of Batman's teachers later became a hero in Gotham. Her real name is Cassandra Cain. What alias has she used as a hero?

- ○ **A.** The Black Canary
- ○ **B.** Batgirl
- ○ **C.** The Black Bat
- ○ **D.** B and C

40. Superman once entrusted Batman with Kryptonite. Why?

- ○ **A.** He believed Batman could find a way to cure Kryptonite poisoning.
- ○ **B.** He believed that if he ever lost control, Batman would be the only friend willing to put him down.
- ○ **C.** Batman had been poisoned by a rare disease that could only be cured by Kryptonite radiation.
- ○ **D.** It was a Christmas gift, the only thing Bruce Wayne didn't already own.

41. The Dark Ranger was inspired by Batman to become a hero. In what country does he operate?

---

42. What was the name of the Dark Ranger's young sidekick?

DIVERSE FRIENDSHIPS

It may seem odd at first that Batman joins forces with alien policemen, shape-shifting Martians, magically empowered warriors, demons, and atomic heroes who can warp matter. But if you think about it, there's absolutely no reason why it shouldn't happen. Thousands of action and adventure films have featured a normal human being who must fight alongside or against some supernatural or science fiction menace. In the world of DC Comics, Batman often takes the place of that normal person. He just happens to be better prepared.

43. Batman has temporarily assumed the powers of which superhero?

○ **A.** Hawkman

○ **B.** Superman

○ **C.** Green Lantern

○ **D.** All of the above

44. Barbara Gordon was the first true Batgirl of Gotham City. For some time though, she used a different alias. What was it?

_____

45. What is the name of the martial artist whom Batman has considered a longtime ally and who has also trained Vic Sage (the original Question) and Barbara Gordon?

○ **A.** Shang Chi

○ **B.** Bronze Tiger

○ **C.** Richard Dragon

○ **D.** Lady Shiva

46. The second Batwoman has a cousin Bette who occasionally operates as a costumed vigilante. What is her heroic name?

_____

47. The Huntress is a vigilante who also calls Gotham City her home. When she was first introduced in the 1970s, readers saw that she was really . . .

_____

48. When Dick Grayson grew older, he took on the alias Nightwing. This named had been used by another hero in the past. Where was that hero from?

_____

49. Which of these costumed ladies has Dick Grayson _not_ dated?

○ **A.** Barbara Gordon, Batgirl

○ **B.** Donna Troy, Wonder Girl

○ **C.** Princess Koriand'r, Starfire

○ **D.** He's dated all of them.

THE BAT-FAMILY

Some may find it odd that a self-professed loner such as Batman would constantly surround himself with agents and teenage apprentices. But considering the character's past, this makes sense. Batman spent time training in the East and learning from ninja shadow masters, many of whom expressed the belief that it is an expert's obligation to train someone else, preparing for the eventuality of death so the hero's knowledge and philosophy will not be lost. In a world of superhumans, sorcerers, serial killers, and alien conquerors, the Dark Knight is all too aware of his own mortality. Besides, as an orphan, perhaps some part of him simply wants to create his own family.

50. Batman has worked alongside an altruistic vampire who inhabits the DC Universe. What is this vampire's name?

51. Batman has shared a few adventures with one of Earth's elemental avatars. This character has been the star of films, live-action television, and cartoons. Who was it?

52. In one story, Wayne Enterprises bought Garrick Laboratories. Who owned this small scientific research company?

- ○ **A.** The original Mr. Terrific
- ○ **B.** The original Flash
- ○ **C.** The original Starman
- ○ **D.** Aquaman

53. In the 1990s, Robin drove a personalized car similar to the Batmobile. What did he call this vehicle?

54. In the pages of *Batman, Inc.*, it was revealed that the original Batwoman's maiden name was . . .

ALWAYS BE PREPARED

Batman's friend Harvey Dent began as a crusading district attorney, only to later be corrupted by the demons of childhood abuse, pent-up rage, and the traumatic incident that left half his face scarred. Over the years, the Dark Knight saw other heroes either turn against their former desire for justice or fall under the sway of some terrible villain. In response, Batman has spent years studying other superheroes, designing plans and weapons to immobilize or capture them if they ever go rogue. As for himself, if he ever goes rogue, Batman trusts that allies like Superman, Wonder Woman, and the Justice League can stop him.

55. Though Batman is considered to be the "world's greatest detective," one of his Justice League teammates is considered to be an investigator of almost equal skill. Who is this hero?

_____

56. Dick Grayson chose "Robin" as his superhero alias. What was the original reason for this?

- ○ **A.** His mother nicknamed him Robin since he once leaped through the air to save his brother, as if he could fly.
- ○ **B.** He intended to emulate Robin Hood.
- ○ **C.** His mother nicknamed him Robin because he was born on the first day of spring.
- ○ **D.** His mother nicknamed him Red Robin because he could never sit still and was constantly "bob-bob-bobbing along."

57. Before she became the second vigilante to be called the Question, Reneé Montoya worked for what organization?

_____

58. What is the name of the test that each Robin must go through as a final exam?

_____

59. One of Batman's trusted allies (and a former teammate) is the woman called Katana. What belief concerning her sword does Katana hold that sometimes disturbs those around her?

_____

60. During a Justice League adventure entitled *The Obsidian Age*, the team was lost in the past and believed to be dead. How did a new team form?

- ○ **A.** Batman had installed a program to activate if the team had been missing for some time, a program which sought out heroes he had pre-selected for a new League.

- ○ **B.** Batman had gotten a message out to the sorcerer Doctor Fate, who sensed what warriors would be needed to save the Leaguers from the past.

- ○ **C.** Batman carved messages into cave walls, knowing they would remain for centuries and be found by his allies in the future.

- ○ **D.** Batman had left a letter to Alfred to be opened if he and the League didn't return, with instructions of who he trusted to form a new team and save the day.

61. What is Kate Kane's middle name? _____

NOT A SIDEKICK

While the Bat-Girl of the 1950s was meant to be a humorous take on a girl pining after Robin, Barbara Gordon was a true hero. When she became Batgirl, it was for altruistic reasons, not because of vengeance. Furthermore, while she sometimes got help and further training from Batman, she was an independent hero. Since then, heroes who take up the mantle of Batgirl may be allies of Batman and may act as his agents for the occasional mission, but they are never his sidekicks.

62. When he first met and fell for the original Batwoman, the Dark Knight believed she was simply a circus owner, film director, and thrill-seeker who had chosen to become a costumed hero for the risk (and maybe for his attention). It turned out she had a hidden agenda. What was it?

○ **A.** Batwoman was an agent of Ra's al Ghul's, sent to get close to the Batman and sway him to joining Ra's side.

○ **B.** Batwoman was an agent of Spyral, a black ops organization that wanted her to learn the true identity of Batman.

○ **C.** Batwoman was actually an alternate version of Catwoman who lived in a parallel universe and had somehow been trapped in the mainstream DC Universe.

○ **D.** Batwoman was Robin's aunt and got close to Batman in order to make sure he was taking care of her nephew.

63. A circus acrobat who wore haunting makeup and called himself the Deadman was later murdered. His ghost now walks the Earth, and he has befriended Batman, able to assist in the fight for justice by temporarily possessing the bodies of the living. When he was alive, what was his name?

_____

64. The Deadman was murdered by a man named Hook. What organization was Hook working for?

_____

65. What is the name of the Deadman's brother? _____

66. Which of Batman's allies has night vision, superhuman strength, bullet-resistant skin, hypnotic abilities, and has served as King of Atlantis?

_____

67. Rory Reagan is the supernatural vigilante called Ragman. What is the terrible secret Batman learned behind the Ragman's patchwork costume?

_____

68. One of Batman's agents pretended to be a gang leader in Gotham and was named after a figure in Greek mythology. What was he called?

_____

69. In Gotham City, there is a private detective who walks with a cane and has helped out the Dark Knight on several cases. What is his name?

_____

70. One of Batman's allies is an android with elemental powers. What is his colorful alias?

_____

71. Batman once went on a date with the hero Vixen. What does Vixen's Tantu Totem amulet allow her to do?

_____

72. During what JLA story arc did Batman and Wonder Woman finally have their first kiss?

_____

WONDER WOMAN

In the DC Universe, Superman, Batman, and Wonder Woman are occasionally referred to as the Trinity. The Dark Knight and the Amazon Warrior Princess didn't have a lot of team-ups on their own until the twenty-first century. Since then, the two have realized how much they have in common. Both are warriors—one an American aristocrat, one a princess of a magical island—always seeking to master new challenges. Several times, the two have shown a trust in each other they do not share with their colleagues. After finally experiencing a kiss, the two used a machine to explore possible futures of what might happen if they were to unite. In the end, they have chosen to remain friends, but readers constantly wonder what might happen one day . . .

Chapter 2 Answer Key

1. Hal Jordan, Green Lantern.
2. D.
3. Leslie Thompkins.
4. C.
5. D.
6. C.
7. Superman.
8. The Creeper.
9. C.
10. John Zatara.
11. Knight and Squire.
12. Flying Fox.
13. B (Dick Grayson, Jason Todd, Tim Drake, Stephanie Brown, Damian Wayne).
14. It was brought to light that she was a homosexual and the military still had the "don't ask, don't tell" policy.
15. Nightrunner.
16. True.
17. Teen Titans.
18. Kid Flash (Wally West) and Aqualad (Garth).
19. B.
20. True.
21. Martian Manhunter, in his identity of Detective John Jones.
22. The tires from the Batmobile.
23. D.
24. Barry Allen.
25. Alan Scott, Green Lantern.
26. A.
27. Kryptonian.
28. Daredevil.
29. D.
30. Man of Bats.
31. Raven Red.
32. C.
33. Her father, Colonel Jake Kane.
34. True.
35. C.
36. Crime Alley.
37. D.
38. Batwing.
39. D.
40. B.
41. Australia.
42. Scout.
43. D.
44. Oracle.
45. C.
46. Flamebird.
47. Helena Wayne, daughter of the Batman and Catwoman who live on Earth-2.
48. Krypton.
49. B.
50. Andrew Bennet.
51. Swamp Thing.
52. B.
53. The Redbird.
54. Katherine Webb.
55. Ralph Dibney, Elongated Man.
56. B (though all the other explanations have been used at some time or another).
57. The GCPD.
58. The Gauntlet.
59. She believes the spirit of her dead husband inhabits her sword.

60. A.

61. Rebecca.

62. B.

63. Boston Brand.

64. Ra's al Ghul's League of Assassins (League of Shadows is acceptable).

65. Cleveland Brand.

66. Aquaman.

67. Each patch is a damned soul bound to his costume and giving him power.

68. Orpheus.

69. Jason Bard.

70. Red Tornado.

71. She gets the powers of whatever animal she focuses on.

72. *JLA: Obsidian Age.*

Score Your Bat-Knowledge!

In this section, there are 72 possible right answers.

If you got 0–34 right, you're no ally of the Dark Knight. You're likely not even a loose acquaintance of his.

If you got 35–56 right, you're fairly familiar with Batman's most obvious heroic allies, but you might want to look up the other ones too.

If you got 57–72 right, congratulations! You are truly an agent of the bat, ready to join forces with a wide variety of heroes whenever the call goes out!

CHAPTER 3

THE VILLAINS

Fans love Batman's world for its villains as well as its heroes. They're intrigued by the counterculture creatures of chaos such as the Joker, Two-Face, Poison Ivy, and Clayface. Batman shows his true formidability and versatility, leaving a faceoff with Gotham's mobs to deal with superpowered monsters, close a case of serial killer clowns, and then join forces with the Justice League against evil computer minds from the far future.

These villains are as colorful and adaptable as the Dark Knight himself. The Joker has been reinterpreted time and time again, reflecting the different approaches and tastes of his writers. Catwoman skirts the line between a criminal who preys on property rather than the innocent and someone who could be a genuine hero if she so chose.

Are you brave enough to walk through the shadowy streets of Gotham City and find out just how much you know about its most famous inhabitants?

1. In the comics, what is the Joker's real name?

_____

2. What is Ra's al Ghul's nickname for Batman?

- ○ **A.** The Knight
- ○ **B.** The Heir
- ○ **C.** My Great Student
- ○ **D.** The Detective

3. Harleen Quinzel is now known as Harley Quinn. But in the 1940s, another woman donned a costume and called herself Harlequin, committing crimes to gain the attention of a certain masked hero. Which superhero did this earlier Harlequin fight?

_____

4. The second criminal to use the name Harlequin in DC Comics adopted this alias during a brief time when she served alongside the Teen Titans. What is her real name?

_____

5. Apart from the Joker, what other now-famous Gotham City criminal appeared in _Batman_ #1 (1940)?

- ○ **A.** Scarecrow
- ○ **B.** Two-Face
- ○ **C.** The Penguin
- ○ **D.** Catwoman

IT'S ALL BATMAN'S FAULT!

Batman was the first character to give comic books the supervillain. In the 1930s, heroes fought strange menaces, deformed monsters, and mad scientists, but costumes and strange masks weren't usually involved. It was not until 1940 that *Batman* #1 brought us theme villains with distinctive costumes (the Joker). By the next year, villains were wearing costumes just like the heroes, even those who used to wear civilian garb such as Catwoman.

6. In the comics, the Riddler legally changed his name to Edward Nygma. What is the Riddler's birth name?

_____

7. What nickname did the criminal from Question 4 originally go by?

_____

8. The woman from Question 4 turned out to be the daughter of someone who lived in a parallel dimension. What name did her father go by?

_____

9. Into what monstrous creature did Dr. Kirk Langstrom transform himself?

_____

10. The villain from Question 5 used a slightly different alias during her or his first appearance. What was this supervillain originally called?

_____

11. One of the first antagonists Batman faced in his career was known as the Monk. Who was this villain?

○ **A.** A sorcerer

○ **B.** A magician who became a terrorist

○ **C.** An assassin working for Ra's al Ghul

○ **D.** A vampire

12. Pamela Isley became the villainous Poison Ivy after a trusted friend and scientist experimented on her. Who was this friend?

_____

13. Early in his career, Batman temporarily used an experimental drug called Venom that increased his strength and resistance to injury. What villain later used this same drug?

_____

14. Ichabod Crane might have been the inspiration for what Batman villain?

_____

15. In 1984, a criminal appeared in Gotham who blamed Gotham City Police Commissioner Gordon for the death of his parents. Who was this twisted villain who in many ways resembled Batman?

_____

16. Many are familiar with the villain Mr. Freeze. When he first appeared though, he used a different name. What was it?

- ○ **A.** Dr. Freeze
- ○ **B.** Captain Cold
- ○ **C.** Freeze-Ray
- ○ **D.** Mr. Zero

THE LADY FROM THE WRONG SIDE

In their first meeting, Batman quickly saw that Catwoman was not just another thief; her talent for disguise and improvisation rivaled his own. When Catwoman was able to miraculously escape at the end of the story, Robin realized that she had been allowed to flee. Since then, it's been a game of cat and flying mouse. Batman often goes easy on the lady since her schemes rarely involve people getting hurt and she seems more interested in thrills than even the money she steals.

17. Julian Day is the true name of what strangely themed criminal?

_____

18. Anthony Lupus turned into what supernatural creature when he fought Batman?

_____

19. Who transformed Lupus into a creature?

_____

20. The true name of the terrorist and cult leader Ra's al Ghul is unknown. The name he uses now is an Arabic title. How does it translate?

○ **A.** The Immortal Demon

○ **B.** The Demon's Head

○ **C.** The Undying Ghost

○ **D.** Wrath of the Demon

○ **E.** The Ghost Who Walks

21. In a 1950s story, which villain once caused Batman to become afraid of bats in all forms, forcing the hero to temporarily adopt the guise of Starman?

_____

22. One of Batman's enemies calls himself Signalman.

○ **A.** True

○ **B.** False

23. One of Batman's enemies is really named Charles Brown. What is his criminal moniker?

_____

24. Batman has fought a group of criminals obsessed with land, sea, and air. Individually, they call themselves Fox, Shark, and Vulture. Together, their team is called . . .

_____

THE TEN-EYED SURGEONS OF THE EMPTY QUARTER

During the 1970s, the Batman of Earth-1 twice fought a strange villain called the Ten-Eyed Man, a U.S. Special Forces veteran who was blinded and then underwent experimental surgery that attached his optic nerves to his fingers. During *Crisis on Infinite Earths*, this villain was deemed too lame to keep around and he was removed from continuity. Twenty years later, writer Grant Morrison revised the concept, introducing a group known as the Ten-Eyed Surgeons (or the "Brotherhood of the Ten-Eyed Men") that operated in Africa's Empty Quarter. These warriors tattooed eyes to their fingers and were known for killing demons of all kinds. When a young Bruce Wayne was training to become Batman, he underwent the trials of the Ten-Eyed brothers, putting his life at risk as they psychically "cut out" the corrupt, self-destructive drives from his soul, ensuring that Batman would be dedicated to justice and not purely vengeance.

25. One of the stranger criminals Batman has faced is a man genetically engineered to be a cross between a bird and a human, with a frail body and hollow bones. What is he called?

_____

26. In various episodes of *Batman: The Brave and the Bold*, a parasitic alien made its way to Earth. What is the name of this creature that has fought Batman and the Justice League many times in the comics?

_____

27. Klaus Kristin was a villain who was born of the union between a human woman and a yeti male. What terrifying criminal name did he go by? (No, we didn't make this up.)

_____

28. What name does Talia al Ghul use professionally in the United States and Europe?

_____

29. The Ten-Eyed Surgeons of the Empty Quarter had a member who went rogue and attempted to kill Bruce Wayne. What was he called?

_____

30. One of Batman's newer enemies shares a name with a beloved character from *The Wind in the Willows* by Kenneth Grahame. Who is this villain?

_____

31. Garfield Lynns is a pyromaniac who at first set fires for money and then decided to set them for sheer joy. To protect himself, he made a suit of body armor that went along with his new criminal nickname. He is . . .

○ **A.** Firebug

○ **B.** Firefly

○ **C.** Pyro

○ **D.** Heatwave

WHAT MIGHT HAVE BEEN

In his first Batman graphic novel, writer Grant Morrison proposed that Arkham Asylum and its inmates could be seen as a metaphor for Batman's mind and the dark demons within. Many of the Dark Knight's foes follow one specific fear we have about ourselves: what we could become if we were pushed far enough or if we stopped caring about morality. Batman can't help but see people such as Two-Face and the Penguin and realize that, if he had been in different circumstances and had less support or less willpower, he could have gone down a similar path.

32. A frequent enemy of the third Robin, Lonnie Machin sees himself as a hero who will help free people from oppression. What does he call himself?

_____

33. This former big game hunter and thief fought Batman while wearing an ancient cloth that was supposedly enchanted to give him multiple lives. Who is he?

_____

34. Actor Basil Karlo (which doesn't sound at all like Boris Karloff) became the first criminal to use this strange alias, which originally referred to the mask that he wore. What is it?

_____

35. This costumed criminal initially attempted to be an anti-Batman who would help criminals, even employing a personalized car and spotlight signal so others could summon him. What insect-themed name did he initially use?

_____

36. Roman Sionis is a former businessman who became a mobster. By what other name is he known?

_____

37. Before he became the Joker, what was the criminal alias used by the Clown Prince of Killers?

_____

38. Who later adopted the Joker's original alias for his own activities?

_____

"WE'RE GOING TO KILL EACH OTHER . . ."

While the moment that birthed his career as Batman filled Bruce Wayne's heart with vengeance, his true calling in life is justice and the protection of life. Several times in his career, he has shown that he hopes for the reformation of many criminals he encounters. When Two-Face seemed to have finally beaten his inner demons, Batman embraced him as a friend again and entrusted him with helping to maintain the safety of Gotham. Even the Joker is not beyond hope. Perhaps Batman's sympathy stems from the fact that he often struggles with his own darkness and capacity for violence.

39. Which serial killer keeps a tally of all his victims by marking his or her own skin?

- ○ **A.** The Calculator
- ○ **B.** The Tally Man
- ○ **C.** Mr. Zsasz
- ○ **D.** Deadshot

40. Basil Karlo later acquired superpowers, turning him into a much more fearsome foe.

- ○ **A.** True
- ○ **B.** False

41. In *Batman: The Animated Series*, who became the Clock King?

- ○ **A.** Temple Fugate
- ○ **B.** Templeton Fugit
- ○ **C.** William Tockman
- ○ **D.** Tick-tock on the clock, Joker's party don't stop

42. Before the appearance of the villain from Question 41, there was another Clock King who usually fought the Green Arrow. What was his real name?

- ○ **A.** Temple Fugate
- ○ **B.** Templeton Fugit
- ○ **C.** Alexander Kronos
- ○ **D.** William Tockman

43. Roman Sionis wore a special mask. Where did he get the material?

_____

44. Arthur Brown is the father of Gotham hero Stephanie Brown. He is also known by what criminal alias? (Hint: Stephanie's first alias was a reference to this alias.)

_____

BANE

Bane's upbringing was the opposite of Bruce Wayne's. Born in a prison, Bane was raised by the rules that exist in such places, where strength and the willingness to kill allow one to survive. As Bruce Wayne took advantage of his wealth and resources to travel the world, Bane's world was surrounded by walls and bars, with nothing to his name save for a teddy bear, Osito, that hid a knife inside its head. Bane was made to be the Dark Knight's opposite number. But he isn't the only skewed reflection . . .

45. Lazlo Valentin is the true identity of what animalistic Batman enemy?

_____

46. What was the alias of the killer who struck once a month in Gotham City during the story *The Long Halloween*?

_____

47. The man who would later be called Dr. Simon Hurt became ageless in the eighteenth century. What was he doing when he encountered the force that made him stop aging?

_____

48. Which criminal mastermind attempted to get a major foothold in Gotham City during the events of the story arc *No Man's Land*?

_____

THE JOKER

So much of the Joker's life is a mystery. But the one story that seems to bear the most weight indicates that he was a man who lost his family one day, a chemist and would-be comedian who decided life had no meaning and that reality was a joke. His crimes are almost a challenge to the universe, that if there is some great plan or some higher power, they wouldn't let him get away with the things he's done. But then comes Batman, who lost his world in one terrible night and yet chose *not* to embrace chaos. The Joker needs Batman to see the joke. He's the straight man of their two-man act, and everyone else is expendable.

49. In *Dark Victory*, a new killer emulated the killer of *The Long Halloween*. What did the newspapers call this new criminal?

_____

50. In *Batman* Vol. 1 #673, how did Joe Chill justify all his crimes, including the murders of Martha and Thomas Wayne?

○ **A.** Class warfare.

○ **B.** He'd been a drug addict and didn't think he could be held responsible for his actions while under the influence.

○ **C.** He regretted the pain he'd caused, but believed he was free of responsibility due to Gotham's economic depression driving him to desperation.

○ **D.** He believed profit was enough of a justification and felt no remorse.

51. The villain Prometheus originally seemed to be a vicious and cunning strategist, only deigning to work with those he deemed to be truly dangerous and intelligent rather than with criminals who completely relied on superpowers. Later, he seemed to become a skilled but not altogether remarkable fighter who was satisfied working as an enforcer for other supervillains. How did writer Sterling Gates explain this change in a special *Faces of Evil* comic?

_____

52. Though many consider him a modern-day villain, Dr. Simon Hurt actually made his first appearance in 1963.

○ **A.** True

○ **B.** False

53. At one point, Batman encountered three false Batmen, each of whom was ready to use lethal force against any who crossed their paths. Who were they?

○ **A.** Three police officers who had undergone training to take Batman's place one day, whether he approved or not.

○ **B.** Three members of Ra's al Ghul's League of Shadows who had been trained specifically to kill Batman with his own methods and weapons.

○ **C.** Three gang members who had become obsessed with Batman but believed he was too soft on crime.

○ **D.** A special military division that had originally been trained to kill Batman and all his apprentices if the hero ever went rogue and became a terrorist.

54. The man known as the Sensei ran the League of Assassins for fifty years before Ra's al Ghul became its true leader.

○ **A.** True

○ **B.** False

RA'S AL GHUL

Though he's walked the Earth for centuries, Ra's al Ghul is not as immortal as he would like others to think. One day, despite his best efforts, the Lazarus Pits will not be able to restore him. He requires an heir and he believes it is Batman, the only one of proper skill, intellect, and willpower. Like Bruce Wayne, Ra's is a man of wealth and influence who decided to use those tools to fight the corruption and evil that plague the Earth. Unlike Bruce, Ra's thinks the best way to save the planet is by killing two-thirds of the humans who "infect" it, allowing Earth to heal while he rules the survivors, who will have no need to fight over dwindling resources.

55. In 1956, a man who was only a few inches tall but had incredible strength pretended to be a new ally of Robin's, only to later reveal that he was a criminal. What was his alias?

_____

56. Nocturna, a criminal introduced in the 1980s, had eyes for Batman. What physical limitation did she possess?

_____

57. Nocturna was born with the limitation mentioned in Question 56.

○ **A.** True

○ **B.** False

58. The criminal Pix had a unique method of controlling others. What did she use to achieve this?

_____

59. In the 1950s, Batman and Robin fought the Gorilla Gang. Who were these strange villains?

○ **A.** A group of criminals from Gorilla City, a society of intelligent gorillas and apes.

○ **B.** A group of criminals who had devolved into gorillas thanks to an experimental temporal energy ray.

○ **C.** A group of gorilla warriors from a future where animals rule and man is nearly extinct.

○ **D.** A common gang of criminals who chose to dress in gorilla costumes to disguise themselves.

60. Before reality was altered during the story *Crisis on Infinite Earths,* what was Poison Ivy's birth name?

_____

61. Query and Echo have been frequent assistants and enforcers to which Gotham City criminal?

_____

62. Who or what executed the villain who called himself the Ratcatcher?

_____

63. A man called Boone operated under the alias of Shrike and considers Nightwing to be a major enemy. How did Boone and Nightwing first meet?

_____

64. Agents of Ra's al Ghul's League of Assassins, occasionally known as the League of Shadows, have trained which of the following superheroes?

○ **A.** Batman

○ **B.** Robin

○ **C.** Bronze Tiger

○ **D.** All of the above

65. Jervis Tech is the mentally disturbed Mad Hatter, often taking over the minds of others with his advanced technology. But for a time, there was a second Mad Hatter with a mustache. What was his main goal and his reason for fighting Batman?

_____

66. In the 853rd century, an older version of Vandal Savage joined forces with an intelligent artificial sun/supercomputer to destroy the Justice League of the modern day and the Justice Legion Alpha of the far future. What was the name of this evil sun-computer?

_____

67. What was the name of the criminal whom Batman faced in his very first comic book story in _Detective Comics #27_?

_____

Chapter 3 Answer Key

1. It's never been revealed, but his first name might be Jack.

2. D.

3. Alan Scott, Green Lantern.

4. Duela Dent.

5. D.

6. Eddie Nashton.

7. Joker's Daughter.

8. The Jokester, a version of the Joker who lives on Earth-3.

9. Man-Bat.

10. The Cat.

11. D.

12. Dr. Jason Woodrue, the Floronic Man.

13. Bane.

14. Jonathan Crane, the Scarecrow.

15. The Wrath.

16. D.

17. Calendar Man.

18. A werewolf.

19. Professor Milo.

20. B.

21. Professor Milo.

22. True.

23. Kite-Man.

24. The Terrible Trio.

25. Skyhook.

26. The Star Conqueror (also called Starro the Conqueror).

27. The Snowman.

28. Talia Head.

29. The Nine-Eyed Man.

30. Mr. Toad.

31. B.

32. Anarky.

33. Catman.

34. Clayface.

35. Killer Moth.

36. Black Mask.

37. The Red Hood.

38. Jason Todd.

39. C.

40. True.

41. A.

42. C.

43. His father's coffin.

44. The Spoiler.

45. Professor Pyg.

46. Holiday.

47. Attempting to summon the demon Barbatos.

48. Lex Luthor.

49. The Hangman.

50. A.

51. There were actually two villains using the name and mask of Prometheus and the second one, apprentice to the first, was the less impressive of the two.

52. True.

53. A.

54. False.

55. Ant-Man.

56. She was incredibly sensitive to light.

57. False.

58. Giving people nannite tattoos.

59. D.

60. Lillian Rose.

61. The Riddler.

62. OMAC units.

63. They both studied under the original Shrike, a member of the League of Assassins.

64. B (Dick Grayson, Tim Drake, and Damian Wayne all underwent training from at least one member of the League, though unlike the others Dick did so after already becoming Robin).

65. He loved collecting hats and wanted Batman's cowl.

66. Solaris.

67. Alfred Stryker.

Score Your Bat-Knowledge!

In this section, there are 67 possible right answers.

If you got 1–25 right, hang your head in shame. You're not worthy to polish the Caped Crusader's trophy cases.

If you got 26–50 right, you know the enemies of Gotham. But look over some of those wanted posters and Arkham files, before you're blind-sided by an enemy's attack

If you got 51–67 right, congratulations! You're a true aficionado of Gotham's greatest criminals. Hopefully, this doesn't make you a target too!

CHAPTER 4

SETTINGS AND LAIRS

Y ou'd think Batman and his rogues' gallery would be enough eye candy for readers. But it doesn't end there. In the comics, films, and cartoons, Gotham City itself is a character. Its sprawling gothic architecture, elevated walkways, and alarmingly large population of gargoyles make it a bleak yet romantic vision of what an American city can be.

Batman's lair is also a part of the mythos that can't be ignored. Batman may refer to it as a place where he works rather than his home, but it seems impossible to picture the character dwelling anywhere else. At times, writers have tried to put him in different locales to provide readers with a change of pace. But inevitably, he returns to Wayne Manor, the home of his parents, and the caves beneath that seem to be the one place where he can truly be himself.

The DC Universe is a big place. How much do you know about it and the many locations Batman has visited and used as a base of operations?

1. The idea that Batman's lair was a cave was first introduced outside of comic books. Where did "The Bat's Cave" make its debut?

_____

2. When it was first founded, what was the area that would one day be called Gotham City actually called?

_____

THE FIRST BATCAVE

When it first appeared (outside of comics), Batman's lair looked like a cave roughly the size of a decent studio apartment with a very practical office desk and chair as the main decoration. Only the shadows of flying bats indicated that this was a natural cave and not some room Batman had decided to customize. In fact, it seemed strange for Batman to be there when his mansion was probably much nicer.

3. Wayne Manor is generally thought to be how far outside Gotham City?

○ **A.** 5 miles

○ **B.** 8 miles

○ **C.** 12 miles

○ **D.** 20 miles

○ **E.** 23 miles

4. In the cartoon *Batman: The Brave and the Bold*, the Dark Knight maintains an auxiliary Batcave, which is hidden in Washington, D.C. Beneath what famous landmark is it located?

_____

5. According to the *Knight's End* story arc, Bruce Wayne's first test as Batman was to leap off a tall Gotham City structure and see if he could save himself from death with his skills and a jump-line. What structure did he leap from?

_____

6. When DC Comics created Arkham Asylum, its name was inspired by what fictional person, place, or thing from the works of H. P. Lovecraft?

_____

7. In the 1990s, Batman helped fund the creation of a lunar base for the Justice League. What was it called?

_____

8. Originally, the lunar base from Question 7 also incorporated technology from what two alien worlds?

_____

9. As mentioned in a question in Chapter 1, Bruce participated in a ritual where he was isolated in a cave for weeks. Outside of what strange city is this cave located?

_____

10. Beneath Arkham Asylum lies one of Batman's satellite Batcaves. In the comics, what is the official designation for this lair?

- ○ **A.** The Narrows Batcave
- ○ **B.** Batcave Gamma
- ○ **C.** Arkham Batcave
- ○ **D.** Batcave Northwest

TRIBE OF THE BAT

Before European settlers began to live in the place that would be Gotham City, a tribe called the Miagani lived in its system of underground caves that would one day house a great hero. These people worshipped the bats that dwelled in their home and spoke of a great bat-god named Barbatos (unrelated to the mythical demon of the same name). During a time travel trip to prehistoric times, Batman himself indirectly inspired the Miagani tribe, forever uniting Gotham with the totem of the bat.

11. In his early adventures, the Green Arrow emulated Batman. What did GA name his own secret lair?

_____

12. According to some role-playing game guides, and based on the accent that Gotham gangster "Matches" Malone is said to have, in what state is Gotham City located?

_____

13. Tim Drake had his own special access to the Batcave, hidden near his family home. What was this alternate entrance?

_____

14. What three famous items occupy the Batcave's trophy room and are most often depicted by comic book artists?

_____

15. Dick Grayson went to a college located 175 miles away from Gotham City. What was the school's name?

_____

16. Due to its high pollution content, Blüdhaven earned what nickname?

_____

17. What great metropolitan newspaper did Bruce Wayne own for several years pre–New 52 Reboot?

_____

18. Who founded Arkham Asylum? _____

19. The Wayne family has its roots in what European country?
- ○ **A.** Scotland
- ○ **B.** England
- ○ **C.** Ireland
- ○ **D.** Norway

PRACTICAL CRIME-FIGHTING HQ

When it was first detailed in the comics, the Batcave seemed to be an underground bunker with just a garage/hangar, a storage room, and a crime lab. One entrance was through Wayne Manor, the other through a nearby old barn. It later evolved into a well-lit command center with two full floors that include a gym, a study, a trophy room, an archive room, elevators, access to an underground river for the Batboat, and a connection to a hollowed-out mountain where the Batplane and Batcopter are kept, with cloud machines rigged to mask their arrivals and departures. Later still, the Batmobile could come and go through a hidden entrance in the side of a large hill, similar to how it was portrayed in the 1960s live-action series.

20. According to official continuity, and an issue of *Batman Chronicles*, what was the very first trophy placed in the Batcave?

_____

21. In the 1970s, Bruce Wayne temporarily left behind Wayne Manor. Where did he move to?

_____

22. For a while, Batman kept a satellite Batcave in Los Angeles. Who primarily used this lair as a base?

_____

23. In pre–New 52 Reboot continuity, Wayne Enterprises acquired Garrick Laboratories. In what city was Garrick Laboratories located?

_____

24. Batman has had several adventures in Metropolis, home of Superman. According to some role-playing game guides, in what state is that city located?

_____

25. In _Detective Comics_ #185 (1952), readers finally learned the actual street address of Wayne Manor. What is it?

○ **A.** 1407 Graymalkin Lane

○ **B.** 1939 Kane Drive

○ **C.** 1007 Mountain Drive

○ **D.** 224 Park Drive

26. "Gotham" used to be a nickname for what real-life place?

_____

27. What penitentiary is local to Gotham City?

_____

28. Gotham City's international airport shares a name with a well-known comic book editor. What is its name?

_____

29. What is the name of Gotham's football team?

_____

30. What was the name of the street where the Waynes were killed?

_____

31. What nickname did this street receive because of the Wayne murders?

_____

32. When Arkham Asylum was founded, for whom was it named?

_____

33. Who made their base in Gotham City's famous Clock Tower?

_____

34. Match the satellite Batcave with its location.

   ___ **A.** Central Batcave   **i.** A boiler room of an abandoned shipping yard.

   ___ **B.** Batcave East   **ii.** A prototype subway station in Old Gotham.

   ___ **C.** Batcave South   **iii.** Beneath Gotham's largest park.

   ___ **D.** Batcave South-Central   **iv.** Abandoned oil refinery.

35. In the mainstream comics, what is the most often-used entrance to the Batcave from Wayne Manor?

_____

36. What is the number combination for the entrance mentioned in Question 35?

_____

37. What is the significance of the number from Question 36?

_____

38. Where was the entrance from Question 35 first seen?

_____

39. In the Earth-1 continuity that existed before the history-altering revisions of _Crisis on Infinite Earths_, what was the original name of the Wayne Foundation?

_____

CHILDHOOD NIGHTMARES

In the 1980s, the Batcave was given a deeper connection to Bruce Wayne's childhood. It was now said that when he was a child of perhaps five or six years old, he fell through a loose patch of Earth and found himself in a small chamber of what would later become the Batcave. For months, he had nightmares of the cave and its bats. Later, when he sat in his study, wondering how to make criminals afraid, his question was answered by a bat that suddenly flew through the window. Inspired by its image, he chose to use it to evoke in others that same fear he had felt as a child.

40. During his time as Batman, Dick Grayson did not use the prime Batcave beneath Wayne Manor but instead used a similar facility Bruce had once kept in the sub-basement of the Wayne Foundation central building. What did Dick call this secret lair?

○ **A.** Batcave II

○ **B.** Neo-Batcave

○ **C.** The Bat-Bunker

○ **D.** Batcave Beta

41. What private academy lies just outside of Gotham and is near the home of Bruce Wayne?

_____

42. The fictional historical figure Burnley Ellsworth was a founding father of a city that acted as home to Batman's ally Jack Knight. What city is this?

_____

43. In the comics, Arkham Asylum is located on an island.

○ **A.** True

○ **B.** False

44. There is a large park in Gotham City. What is it called?

_____

45. For which artist was the park named?

_____

46. What large river separates Gotham City from the mainland of the East Coast?

- ○ **A.** Kane River
- ○ **B.** Gotham River
- ○ **C.** Finger River
- ○ **D.** Sprang River
- ○ **E.** Miller River

47. What is the name of Gotham's major sporting complex?

_____

48. Batman and the Question have both undergone training in a mystical hidden city in the mountains of Tibet. What is the name of this strange city?

_____

49. What is the name of the goddess who watches over the city mentioned in Question 48?

_____

50. Batman's enemy Prometheus made his base in a crooked house. Where was this house located?

_____

A SYMBOLIC HOUSE

When it was first designed, Wayne Manor was built to form a giant W as a symbol of its powerful family. Later on, gardens were added that, if you look at it the right way, create the image of a bat. In *Batman: The Animated Series*, the main section of Wayne Manor was given two points that implied the shape of a bat's ears.

51. Who originally designed Wayne Manor?

_____

52. Though WayneTech is impressive, another research organization is known throughout the world of DC Comics for its study of alien technology and superhumans. The hero Cyborg's father worked there. What is this organization?

_____

53. Long before Bruce Wayne was born, what did his ancestors use the Batcave for?

_____

54. In the late 1990s, Gotham City suffered a massive earthquake during the storyline *Cataclysm*, resulting in massive property damage and loss of life. Who caused this catastrophe?

- ○ **A.** Rictor
- ○ **B.** Quakemaster
- ○ **C.** No one—it was a natural disaster.
- ○ **D.** Ra's al Ghul

55. What two rivers cross through Gotham City itself?

_____

56. Originally, Batman creators Bill Finger and Bob Kane considered Bruce Wayne's adventures as taking place in what city?

_____

SILENT PARTNER

Even when they're not aware of it, Batman seems to like helping other superheroes. When one of his companies purchases a corporation belonging to another hero, he's always made sure that employees are able to keep their jobs and that his fellow heroes are not dismissed. When Oliver Queen could no longer financially support the Justice League's resources, Bruce Wayne stepped in as the secret backer.

57. What is the name of the botanical garden housed in Gotham's largest park?

_____

58. What is another name for the satellite Batcave hidden beneath Los Angeles?

_____

59. Did Dick Grayson graduate from college?

_____

60. Who was the first member of the Wayne family to inhabit Wayne Manor?

_____

61. The city of Blüdhaven is located twenty-three miles from Gotham in what direction?

○ **A.** North

○ **B.** South

○ **C.** West

○ **D.** East

62. According to the story _Batman: Year Two_, what did Bruce Wayne hide in the cornerstone of the Wayne Foundation building?

_____

63. In the cartoon show _Young Justice,_ Gotham City is located in what state?

_____

64. In the animated universe of _Batman: The Animated Series_, and related direct-to-video films, license plates and certain viewed records stated that Gotham City was located in what state?

_____

65. In an episode of *Smallville*, the character Linda Lake jokes that she can see Gotham City from her window in a building in Metropolis. Why would this be literally impossible in the world of the TV show *Smallville*?

_____

66. The map of Gotham used for the 1989 film *Batman* was actually an inverted map of Vancouver, British Columbia, Canada.

○ **A.** True

○ **B.** False

67. As seen in *JLA: Classified* #1, there is a storage chamber in the Batcave where the Dark Knight keeps alien technology and weapons he's collected. What is his nickname for this storage chamber?

_____

68. In the comics, what are the Lazarus Pits?

○ **A.** A mixture of chemicals in pools that must be used only by members of Ra's al Ghul's bloodline.

○ **B.** A mixture of chemicals in pools that Ra's al Ghul must build in certain areas or else it will be lethal.

○ **C.** Naturally occurring pools of unknown chemicals that Ra's al Ghul found and immediately began hiding.

○ **D.** Naturally occurring phenomena that were created by the same meteorite that made Vandal Savage immortal.

69. It has been said that Gotham's inclination toward crime was greatly influenced by the greater corruption in nearby Blüdhaven.

○ **A.** True

○ **B.** False

70. The idea that the Dark Knight keeps a satellite Batcave beneath
Arkham Asylum was specifically invented for the game *Batman:
Arkham Asylum* and then later adapted into the comics.

○ **A.** True

○ **B.** False

71. As audiences got to know the vision of Gotham presented in Tim
Burton's *Batman* film, DC comics produced a three-issue story
that resulted in their version of Gotham City matching up. What
was the story's explanation for Gotham changing its appearance
almost overnight?

_____

SATELLITE CAVES

At first, Batman only created alternate bases (referred to as satellite Batcaves even
if they weren't built inside a cavern) when he needed them. He planned to spend
some time in L.A., so a Batcave was built there. Likewise he built another when he
temporarily moved out of Wayne Manor. But after being blindsided by Bane, who
invaded Wayne Manor and then the main Batcave, Batman realized how vulnerable
he was and spent a couple of weeks building other hidden bases around Gotham
City, as well as secret supply storage units. Just in case . . .

72. Who was the designer of the version of Gotham City that first
appeared in the film *Batman*?

_____

73. *Batman: The Animated Series* provided a different address for Wayne Manor in "The Demon's Quest." What was it?

_____

74. Since the 1980s, Batman's continuity has stated that he attended several colleges, never completing a single semester before moving on to further his education in what he believed was the most effective way. But before then, it was said that Batman attended and graduated from one university. Which one was it?

_____

75. In the original Golden Age continuity, who commissioned the construction of Wayne Manor?

_____

76. The Joker once had a lair with an entrance resembling his face. What did he call this whimsical HQ?

_____

77. In *Batman Begins*, Arkham Asylum is located on an island and is surrounded by clustered apartment buildings and low-rent housing. In that film, what is this area called?

_____

78. In the cartoon series *The Batman*, a rival company to Wayne Industries was introduced. What was it called?

_____

79. Since the 1990s, who was usually depicted as Arkham Asylum's administrative director?

_____

80. In contrast to the comics, who ran Arkham Asylum in _The Batman_?

_____

81. Superman and Batman have been called the World's Finest Team. What is the name of Superman's famous lair, located above the Arctic Circle?

_____

82. How did Superman gain access to his original Arctic lair?

_____

83. In the 1950s, wanting to play a joke on the Man of Steel, how did the Dark Knight enter the hidden Arctic sanctuary?

_____

84. After Bane destroyed much of Arkham Asylum during the events of _Knightfall,_ the asylum inmates were moved to what building, turning it into the new Arkham?

_____

85. Which of Batman's enemies had previously used the building in Question 84 as a base of operations?

_____

86. The Hall of Justice became famous as the headquarters of DC's biggest heroes in the Super Friends cartoons. This HQ was based on what art deco railroad station?

_____

87. Early in his career, Batman was tracking down a criminal known as the Red Hood. At which chemical plant did the Red Hood seemingly meet his demise?

_____

88. The night the Red Hood and Batman fought in a chemical plant, the criminal had actually intended to rob a building next door. What company was based in that building?

_____

HIDDEN ROOMS

Batman is, by his own admission, a control freak. If he has any way of doing it, he'll make sure he has a hideaway in an important place where he can be undetected and watch others. Along with the base beneath Arkham Asylum, which he knows is a trouble spot, Batman once rigged the Justice League teleporters so that, with the right code, you would not be teleported from one base to another but would end up in a hidden room slightly out of phase with reality, which he called the Lounge. He intended this to be a place where he, Superman, and Wonder Woman could discuss Justice League affairs in private.

89. Batman's ally Deadman used to be an acrobat for what circus?

_____

90. When it was finally introduced into the official comics continuity, in what city was the Hall of Justice located?

_____

91. In the _Young Justice_ cartoon show, Batman housed the young heroes in a mountain base. What is it called in the show?

_____

92. In the comics, the HQ mentioned in Question 91 was usually called the Justice Cave. What was its original name, though?

_____

93. At what harbor was the base in Question 91 located?

_____

94. The Justice League had their lunar base and, in the anti-matter universe, the Crime Syndicate had theirs. What was it called?

_____

95. What is the phrase written on the meeting table of the Crime Syndicate of Amerika?

_____

96. In DC Comics a very famous city is kept in a bottle. What is its name?

_____

97. Where was the city of Question 96 originally from?

_____

98. How did the city of Question 96 get into its bottle prison?

_____

99. More than once, Batman has fought against the Rogues. What twin cities do the Rogues normally operate in?

_____

100. The Rogues have been known to visit a place called Avernus Cemetery. What makes this location so special to them?

_____

101. Which superhero team used a brownstone in Gotham City as their HQ for a time?

_____

102. What significance does the prison Peña Duro hold for Batman?

_____

103. The Iceberg Lounge is a front for arms deals and other criminal escapades. Who runs it?

_____

104. It has been said that Gotham City was truly built by four families. The Waynes are one of those families. Name the other three.

_____

105. As "Matches" Malone, Batman briefly allowed himself to be locked up in what prison in Louisiana?

_____

106. What classic film and stage play mentions a place that shares a name with the answer to Question 105?

_____

107. While at the prison mentioned in Question 105, Batman discovered it secretly housed what group?

_____

108. *Batman: The Animated Series* had a different name for Gotham's local prison. What was it called in the show?

_____

109. Worse than Gotham City is the Midwestern den of sin known as Hub City. What strange, non-costume wearing vigilante called this place home?

_____

110. During the crossover event Infinite Crisis, what creature was used to wipe out Blüdhaven?

_____

111. Batman's ally Geo-Force hails from what fictional European country?

_____

POLAR OPPOSITES

A lair can give you insight on how its occupant views his place in the world. Batman houses himself underground, giving off the impression that he is lying in wait to strike while simultaneously implying that he sometimes feels the need to retreat from the world and cut himself off even from the sky. Meanwhile, on a mirror Earth in an anti-matter universe, his double Owlman has been seen operating in a tower that looms over Gotham City, matching his bird motif and allowing him to peer down on the people he considers prey.

112. What position of power does Geo-Force hold in his native land?

_____

113. Batman's ally Aquaman often calls the mythical Atlantis his home. What is the capital city of Atlantis?

114. The Green Lantern Corps involves heroes from all across the universe, each of whom patrols a sector of space filled with many different planets. Which Green Lantern was proud to say he had been trained in combat by Batman?

115. There is another major city of Atlantis called Tritonis. What is the noticeable difference between the people of Tritonis and the people who live in the city mentioned in Question 113?

116. From what world in the Fifth Dimension do Bat-Mite, Qwsp, and Mr. Mxyzptlk apparently come from?

117. When once asked if he were really a powerful being from the Fifth Dimension or just a figment of imagination, what did Bat-Mite reply?

118. As he escaped Darkseid's time exile and made his way back to modern-day Gotham City, Batman found himself in a place outside of space and time. What was the name of this strange facility?

_____

119. When the facility from Question 118 was first introduced, what group called it home?

_____

120. Batman and Superman once located a hidden base for Squad K, a group trained by the military to eliminate Superman if they had to. Beneath what town was Squad K's secret base?

_____

121. At the beginning of the New 52 books, which government-authorized team had just formed and moved into the Hall of Justice?

_____

122. During an adventure with the demon Etrigan, Batman literally went to Hell.

  ◯ **A.** True

  ◯ **B.** False

123. If Batman needs to find a place where mages and sorcerers are gathered, he can always check out which watering hole?

_____

FLYING CAVES

In one of Batman's wackier Golden Age stories, the Dark Knight and Robin operated a large-scale helicopter that acted as a mini HQ. Despite the contradiction in terms, they called this the Flying Batcave. While it was definitely silly and tends to inspire giggles, it also provides another example of Batman's versatility.

124. According to the new DCU continuity, which planet marks Batman's very first trip to another world?

_____

125. What other planet is most often associated with the one mentioned in Question 124?

_____

Chapter 4 Answer Key

1. The 1943 Batman movie serials.
2. Gotham Town.
3. C.
4. The Lincoln Memorial.
5. Wayne Tower.
6. The town of Arkham, Massachusetts.
7. The Watchtower.
8. Mars and Thanagar.
9. Nanda Parbat.
10. D.
11. The ArrowCave.
12. New Jersey.
13. A dry well inside an old barn.
14. A robot T-rex, a giant penny, a giant Joker playing card.
15. Hudson University.
16. Asbestos City.
17. *The Daily Planet.*
18. Amadeus Arkham.
19. A.
20. The robot T-Rex.
21. The penthouse of the Wayne Foundation building.
22. The Outsiders.
23. Keystone City.
24. Delaware.
25. D.
26. New York City.
27. Blackgate.
28. Archie Goodwin International.
29. The Knights.
30. Park Row.
31. Crime Alley.
32. Elizabeth Arkham, Amadeus's mother.
33. Barbara Gordon as Oracle.
34. A-iii, B-iv, C-i, D-ii.
35. A door hidden behind a grandfather clock.
36. The hands must go counter-clockwise to 10:47 P.M.
37. It is the time of death for Martha and Thomas Wayne (his watch cracked when he hit the ground).
38. In the 1943 Batman serials.
39. The Alfred Memorial Foundation.
40. C.
41. Bristol Academy.
42. Opal City.
43. True.
44. Robinson Park.
45. Jerry Robinson.
46. B.
47. Knights Dome.
48. Nanda Parbat.
49. Rama Kushna.
50. The Ghost Zone (which may or may not be part of the Phantom Zone).
51. Nathan van Derm.
52. S.T.A.R. Labs.
53. A station on the Underground Railroad.
54. C.
55. Spring River and Finger River.
56. Los Angeles.
57. Wayne Botanical Garden.
58. Batcave West.
59. No.
60. Darius Wayne.

61. B.

62. The gun that killed his parents.

63. Connecticut.

64. New York.

65. Gotham is consistently depicted as a city on the Eastern seaboard, and the TV series *Smallville* placed Metropolis as being a three-hour drive from Smallville, Kansas.

66. True.

67. The Sci-Fi Closet.

68. B.

69. True.

70. False.

71. A bomber destroyed many of Gotham's modern buildings, letting older architecture come into view again.

72. Anton Furst.

73. 1007 Mountain Drive.

74. Gotham College.

75. Bruce Wayne.

76. Ha-Hacienda.

77. The Narrows.

78. GothCorp.

79. Jeremiah Arkham.

80. Prof. Hugo Strange.

81. The Fortress of Solitude.

82. He lifted a giant key, disguised as an airplane marker, to open a door so heavy that only someone near his strength level could move it.

83. Batman hid inside the giant key.

84. Mercey Mansion.

85. The Joker.

86. Union Terminal in Cincinnati.

87. Ace Chemicals.

88. The Monarch Playing Card Company.

89. Hill Bros.

90. Washington, D.C.

91. Mount Justice.

92. The Secret Sanctuary.

93. Happy Harbor, Rhode Island.

94. The Panopticon.

95. Cui Bono.

96. Kandor.

97. Krypton.

98. The villain Brainiac shrunk it and added it to his collection of cities from the worlds he visits.

99. Central City and Keystone City.

100. It's a hidden cemetery for enemies of the Flash.

101. The Justice Society of America.

102. It's the birthplace of Bane.

103. The Penguin.

104. The Cobblepots, the Elliots, and the Kanes.

105. Belle Reve.

106. *A Streetcar Named Desire.*

107. Task Force X, also known as the Suicide Squad.

108. Stonegate.

109. Vic Sage, the first Question.

110. Chemo.

111. Markovia.

112. He is the prince.

113. Poseidonis.

114. Kyle Rayner.

115. People from Poseidonis look like humans, with their gills not obvious on sight, whereas people from Tritonis are literal mermaids and mermen.

116. Zrrf.

117. He said imagination *is* the Fifth Dimension.

118. Vanishing Point.

119. The Linear Men.

120. Smallville, Kansas.

121. Justice League International.

122. True.

123. The Oblivion Bar.

124. Apokolips.

125. New Genesis.

Score Your Bat-Knowledge!

In this section, there are 128 possible right answers.

If you got 1–64 right, hang your head in shame, you tourist. You've got a lot to learn about the DC Universe and Gotham City.

If you got 65–94 right, you've definitely visited Gotham and the DCU on several occasions, but you may want to pay more attention during your next adventure there.

If you got 95–128 right, congratulations! You deserve your own Batcave!

CHAPTER 5

DAILIES, COMICS, AND BOOKS

*T*hough Batman was birthed in the comic books, that isn't the medium of choice for some people. The page layouts, pacing, and visual effects can be jarring. Others simply prefer a different kind of storytelling, perhaps one where the installments come every day rather than every month—for instance, in the pages of a daily newspaper. Audio plays can make for a nice change of pace as well. And then there are readers who enjoy the idea of characters such as Batman and the Joker, but have trouble taking cartoon images seriously and prefer their adventure in prose form.

Some of the novels, audio plays, and daily strips are based on stories that already appeared in the comic books. Some present new stories with familiar characters. Some are completely original, throwing Batman against enemies he'd never encountered before and, possibly, never would again. See how much you know about these other interpretations of the Dark Knight of Gotham City.

1. The BBC radio play *Batman: The Lazarus Syndrome* takes place on a special anniversary Batman celebrates. What does this anniversary commemorate?

_____

2. Most of the BBC radio play *Knightfall* is based on the saga of the same name. But the first several scenes are based on what mini-series illustrated by Joe Quesada?

_____

3. The opening scene of *Batman: The Lazarus Syndrome* takes place in what famous place in Gotham City?

_____

4. The BBC radio production of *Knightfall* featured Mark Hamill as the Joker.

○ **A.** True

○ **B.** False

FRIENDSHIPS

In the novelization of *Crisis on Infinite Earths*, writer Marv Wolfman explored the differences between superheroes who were colleagues and those who were friends. Batman seemed to have a stronger friendship with the Flash, the Martian Manhunter, and the Hawkman of Thanagar. Barry Allen, the Flash, believed this was due to the fact that he was a CSI, Martian Manhunter was a police detective and then a private investigator, and Hawkman was an alien police officer. Batman respected that each was devoted to justice in all aspects of his life.

5. What actor from multiple live-action Batman films reprised his role in the BBC's *Batman: The Lazarus Syndrome*?

_____

6. *Batman: The Lazarus Syndrome* was broadcast to commemorate what event?

_____

7. Which writer penned both the novel *Batman/Superman: Enemies & Allies* and *The Last Days of Krypton*?

_____

8. In *Batman/Superman: Enemies & Allies*, Bruce Wayne has allowed the Thomas and Martha Wayne Memorial Park to fall into disrepair. Why?

_____

9. In the novel *Batman/Superman: Enemies & Allies* the company LexCorp uses a different name. What is it called instead?

_____

10. In *Batman: Inferno*, someone is masquerading as the Dark Knight. Who is it?

_____

11. What is the name of the pyromaniac who stalks the pages of *Batman: Inferno*?

_____

12. In *Batman: Dead White*, the Dark Knight of Gotham faced a group of white supremacists. Who was the leader of this group?

_____

13. In the novel *The Batman Murder*, several deceased victims are found. What common element do the murder victims share?

_____

14. In the book *Batman: To Stalk a Spectre*, a witness in a major case against a crime lord is targeted by an assassin and put under federal protection. What action does Batman take to make sure the witness remains safe?

_____

EXPANDED ORIGINS

Batman: To Stalk a Spectre delved deeper into Batman's thoughts and feelings during the moment when a bat crashed through the window of his study, inspiring the guise he would adopt to frighten criminals. When Bruce Wayne's hand touched the intruding creature, he experienced *satori*, a deeper understanding and vision of one's own nature. He saw his connection to the bat and understood that this would be his totem forever.

15. In the Batman daily newspaper strips in the 1940s, where in Wayne Manor was the hidden access to the Batcave?

_____

16. As can be seen in *Batman: The Sunday Classics*, a female thief disguises herself as a man at one point. What gives her away to Batman's keen detective skills?

_____

17. Though the Batman Sunday comic strips were all credited to Bob Kane, which DC artist who co-created Starman did a lot of the art for these stories?

_____

18. Which Batman novel deals with a demonic car cruising through Gotham's streets and running people down?

_____

19. In one Batman Sunday strip story, the Penguin asked for Batman's help in convincing a woman that he was not a criminal. Who was she?

○ **A.** The Penguin's sister

○ **B.** The Penguin's aunt

○ **C.** The Penguin's mother

○ **D.** The Penguin's cousin

20. In the Batman Sunday strip story "Gotham's Cleverest Criminal," the Joker escapes prison because a criminal is stealing his glory as the smartest fiend. What name does this other criminal go by?

_____

21. In the continuity of the Batman Sunday comic strips, Two-Face is not a district attorney before he becomes a criminal. What profession does he hold instead?

_____

22. What is Two-Face's real name in the Batman Sunday comic strips?

_____

23. In *Batman: To Stalk a Spectre*, readers learned that Gotham has its own version of New York City's Guardian Angels. What is the Gotham group called?

_____

24. Which novel features Batman investigating the source of a fear toxin, only to find that the Scarecrow and all the usual suspects are still locked up in Arkham Asylum?

_____

25. In 1996, a novel was published that involved Batman discovering that his mother had focused quite a bit of her social work on fighting sexual abuse against children. What is the title of the novel?

_____

26. The novel from Question 25 implied that Joe Chill targeted the Waynes because he had been hired by a group of pedophiles who wanted Martha Wayne dead.

○ **A.** True

○ **B.** False

27. The novel from Question 25 is by a crime novelist who also works as an attorney who exclusively represents children and youths. What is his name?

_____

28. Which of these epic stories featuring Batman (sometimes among other heroes) has not been the subject of a novelization?

○ **A.** *Batman: Contagion*

○ **B.** *Batman: Knight's End*

○ **C.** *Final Crisis*

○ **D.** *Crisis on Infinite Earths*

FREEDOM FROM CONTINUITY

Although many tie-in novels today attempt to line up the story with the canon of the comics, previous collections played fast and loose with things. Some stories depicted a Batman similar to modern comics, some seemed more akin to the 1960s portrayal by Adam West, others placed him in a supernatural/horror atmosphere not usually seen in his stories. With the "anything goes" attitude, anthologies could appeal to a wide variety of audiences.

29. The author of the novelization *Batman: No Man's Land*, opened the book by telling the story from whose point of view?

_____

30. Which two costumed heroes were present in Gotham for at least a few of the *No Man's Land* comics but were dropped entirely from the novelization?

_____

31. The novel *DC Universe: Helltown* features Batman and the assassin Lady Shiva. The book presents a new, expanded origin story for which character of the DCU?

_____

32. *DC Universe: Helltown* contradicted much of the Question's origin and backstory in DC Comics, even though it was written by Dennis O'Neil, who introduced the character into DC and wrote his adventures for years.

○ **A.** True

○ **B.** False

33. In *DC Universe: Inheritance*, which former teen sidekick is said to have belonged to a band called the Great Frog?

_____

34. Match the group with the *DC Universe* novel that had these characters join forces.

___ **A.** Batman, Aquaman, Green Arrow   **i.** *Last Sons*

___ **B.** Lobo, Superman, Martian Manhunter   **ii.** *Trail of Time*

___ **C.** Superman, Zatanna, Etrigan   **iii.** *Inheritance*

35. After the long saga that began with *Knightfall*, the comics had Bruce Wayne determined to become Batman again after taking the mantle back from his temporary replacement Azrael. This allowed the warrior to go free in the hopes that he would one day make up for his sins as the ersatz Dark Knight. But the novelization *Knightfall* had what slightly different ending?

○ **A.** Bruce told Tim Drake to call Dick Grayson so he could permanently turn over the role of Batman and find a new life for himself.

○ **B.** Bruce told Tim Drake that he was not sure what his future was or if he would indeed become Batman again.

○ **C.** Bruce had Azrael committed to Arkham Asylum, deciding he was simply too dangerous to be allowed to roam freely.

○ **D.** Bruce began a new worldwide organization of Batmen, jokingly calling it "Batman, Inc."

EMPHASIS ON DETECTIVE

Because of the pacing of a daily newspaper strip, the Batman dailies were not as big on drawn-out fight scenes and car chases as the comics sometimes were. The Batman of the dailies was a detective first and foremost. Nearly every three- or four-panel segment would end with the Dark Knight discovering a new clue or a new plot twist.

36. In the BBC radio play *Batman: The Lazarus Syndrome*, who is to be given a cassette from Batman in the event of his death?

_____

37. What does the cassette from Question 36 reveal?

_____

38. In the Batman daily newspaper strips of the 1940s, a police officer impersonates Batman to help stop illegal operations concerning the selling of fur. Why did Batman allow this?

_____

39. Although he wrote the novelizations of both *Countdown* and *Final Crisis*, author Greg Cox had to largely ignore the events of the first book when he wrote the second, since the original *Final Crisis* comics and related material contradicted too much of the *Countdown* comics.

○ **A.** True

○ **B.** False

40. What happened to the police officer from Question 38?

_____

41. Although he is mentioned in the BBC radio play *Batman: The Lazarus Syndrome,* Hugo Strange never appears in the story.

   ○ **A.** True

   ○ **B.** False

42. At the time of the BBC radio play *Batman: The Lazarus Syndrome,* Harvey Dent is still Gotham's district attorney and hasn't become Two-Face yet.

   ○ **A.** True

   ○ **B.** False

43. In the novelization of *Crisis on Infinite Earths*, Batman sees what seems to be a ghostly vision of which Justice League comrade who has been missing for some time?

_____

44. The novel *JLA: Exterminators* features Batman and the Justice League investigating an outbreak of what among Earth's population?

_____

IT'S ALL IN THE SETUP

Just as Batman's methods were now paced to create a whodunit atmosphere, some of his famous villains now focused on suspense rather than assaulting readers with sudden, garish crimes. For instance, one day's segment featured a captured Joker declaring that he had all the tools he needed to escape his imprisonment. Readers then saw him holding only a nail, a match, a cigarette stub, and a paper bag, and had to wait another day to learn how these items would free him from his guards.

45. The novelization for *Batman: No Man's Land* has a completely different ending from the comics because author Greg Rucka did not know how his colleagues at DC Comics were going to end it.

○ **A.** True

○ **B.** False

46. Which major superhero team arrived to help out the Justice League in *JLA: Exterminators*?

_____

47. Which well-known Batman comic writer wrote the novel *Justice League of America—Batman: The Stone King*?

_____

48. In the novel mentioned in Question 47, after the Justice League stops a dam from bursting, what strange structure is revealed?

_____

49. Which anthology contains a Batman story penned by Isaac Asimov, who has been called the "grandfather of science fiction"?

○ **A.** *Tales of the Batman*

○ **B.** *The Adventures of the Batman*

○ **C.** *The Further Adventures of Batman,* Vol. 3

○ **D.** *Legends of the Batman*

SWEAT THE DETAILS

Most comic book artists don't spend a lot of time detailing things such as the construction of Batman's body armor or the materials used to make a batarang. Readers see that the body armor and weapons work and they move on with the story. But in tie-in novels, an entire paragraph or two might be spent explaining the range of Batman's weapons before he puts them into action.

50. The only Batman villain to receive an anthology book with stories focused on him is the Joker.

○ **A.** True

○ **B.** False

Chapter 5 Answer Key

1. The death of his parents.
2. *Batman: Sword of Azrael.*
3. Crime Alley.
4. False.
5. Michael Gough.
6. The fiftieth anniversary of Batman.
7. Kevin J. Anderson.
8. Batman considered the disreputable park as bait, bringing in criminals that he could watch and interrogate.
9. LuthorCorp.
10. The Joker.
11. Enfer.
12. White Eyes.
13. They are all found wearing Batman costumes.
14. Batman kidnaps the witness and keeps her in the Batcave.
15. It is behind a book shelf.
16. He saw a "man" who had no Adam's apple.
17. Jack Burnley.
18. *Batman: Captured by the Engines.*
19. C.
20. Sparrow.
21. Actor.
22. Harvey Apollo.
23. The Green Dragons.
24. *Batman: Fear Itself.*
25. *Batman: The Ultimate Evil.*
26. True.
27. Andrew Vachss.
28. A.
29. Oracle.
30. Azrael and Superman.
31. Vic Sage, The Question.
32. True.
33. Arsenal, formerly known as Speedy, sometimes called Red Arrow (any of these answers work).
34. A-iii, B-i, C-ii.
35. B.
36. Commissioner Gordon.
37. Batman's true identity.
38. He was injured and temporarily immobilized.
39. True.
40. He was killed while still dressed as Batman.
41. True.
42. False.
43. Barry Allen, the Flash.
44. Superpowers.
45. False.
46. The Justice Society of America.
47. Alan Grant.
48. A stone pyramid.
49. A.
50. False.

Score Your Bat-Knowledge!

In this section, there are 52 possible right answers.

If you got 1–22 right, you need to remember that comic books are not the only reading materials out there.

If you got 23–37 right, you've explored some of Batman's other interpretations, but you may be missing out on some of the great stuff like the audio plays.

If you got 38–52 right, congratulations! You are truly a reader in the best sense of the word and you appreciate the challenges of different media!

CHAPTER 6

FILM, TV, AND VIDEOGAMES

*B*atman has been interpreted across all media. With his distinctive disguise, dark settings, and a rogues' gallery of colorful and sometimes disfigured criminals, it's no wonder that the Caped Crusader's stories lend themselves to great visuals in cartoon, television, and film. The striking landscape of Gotham has been reinterpreted time and time again. It may look like a city stuck in time, with art deco mashed against neo-gothic architecture. It may seem like a twisted version of the darkest days of New York City and Chicago. It may seem like a strange vision of a bleak future. But in the end, it will always be, first and foremost, the home of Batman.

Batman himself is just as adaptable as his city. Is he a dark vigilante who will occasionally kill his enemies and throw their henchmen off rooftops? Is he a modern-day samurai who pretends to be a demon but refuses to kill? Is he a recognized law official, operating in broad daylight while wearing tights and a cape? It can depend entirely on which version of the mythos you visit. And sometimes, recent adaptations find their roots in earlier comics that inspired the writers and artists.

With their versatility for interpretation, it's no wonder the Batman and his cast have displayed such longevity. Whether you prefer the campy Adam West live-action Batman TV series of the 1960s, the dark atmosphere of *Batman: The Animated Series*, or the reboot film franchise directed by Chris Nolan, a true fan can find something to appreciate about each interpretation. Well, except for the movie *Batman & Robin* maybe . . .

NOTE:

For clarity's sake, in this chapter the 1966 film which is sometimes referred to as *Batman* or *Batman: The Movie*, will be called *Batman: The Movie*. The simpler title *Batman* will refer to the 1989 feature film. Neither of these should be confused with the WB cartoon series entitled *The Batman*. On Fox, *Batman: The Animated Series* was later retitled *The Adventures of Batman & Robin* and then evolved into *The New Batman Adventures*. However, all three of these shows are commonly referred to under the umbrella name of *Batman: TAS* and are sold on DVD as one continuous program.

1. In the 1960s live-action Batman series, how did one access the Batcave from Wayne Manor?

_____

2. In *Batman Begins*, Bruce Wayne sprays his suit with black latex paint. Why?

○ **A.** He needs it to be darker in order to seem more like a living shadow.

○ **B.** He wants to make the suit's weak points less obvious by painting over them.

○ **C.** Latex paint hides heat, making Batman invisible to infrared detection.

○ **D.** It helps the suit's insulation so he won't get so cold from the high winds one would encounter while gliding from skyscrapers.

3. In the comics, the Penguin is often depicted with a monocle perched at his eye. What does he wear in its place in *Batman: Arkham City*?

_____

4. Match the actor with the show or feature that featured them as Batman.

__ **A.** William Baldwin	i. *Super Friends*
__ **B.** Diedrich Bader	ii. *The Batman*
__ **C.** Will Friedle	iii. *Super Friends: The Legendary Super Powers Show*
__ **D.** Rino Romano	iv. *Justice League: Crisis on Two Earths*
__ **E.** Olan Soule	v. *Batman Beyond*
__ **F.** Adam West	vi. *Batman: The Brave and the Bold*

5. The game *Batman: Dark Tomorrow* begins with a gang war in Gotham City. On one side are Scarface and the Ventriloquist. Who is on the other side?

_____

6. In *LEGO Batman: The Video Game*, what activity does Clayface enjoy while imprisoned at Arkham Asylum?

_____

7. *Batman: Arkham City* portrays Robin as having a hood attached to his cape. This is the first time he was seen wearing a hood, and it was later adapted into the comics.

○ **A.** True

○ **B.** False

THE FIRST FILM FRANCHISE

Batman made his first appearances on the silver screen in 1940s movie serials. There was later *Batman: The Movie*, which was released between the first and second seasons of the popular show starring Adam West and Burt Ward. But when many talk about "the first Batman film," they mean the 1989 movie directed by Tim Burton, starring Michael Keaton and Jack Nicholson. Likewise, the "first Batman film franchise" refers to it and the four sequels it spawned.

8. In *Batman Begins* and *The Dark Knight*, Bruce's voice is noticeably different when he dons his costume. What is the story reason for this?

○ **A.** In *Batman Begins*, Bruce learned many secrets of theatricality from the League of Shadows. A cut scene showed him learning from the League members how to alter his voice to sound more demonic and inhuman.

○ **B.** In *Batman Begins*, you can see Batman installing small pieces of technology into his cowl while he speaks with Alfred. One of these devices amplifies and alters his voice.

○ **C.** A cut scene from *Batman Begins* would have had Bruce testing different voices with Alfred, a gifted mimic, until finding one that his computer couldn't accurately recognize as his own.

○ **D.** There was no explanation for this. Director Chris Nolan simply added the vocal distortion in post-production at the last minute.

9. Peter MacNicol has appeared in *Ally McBeal*, *Ghostbusters 2*, and *Spectacular Spider-Man*. Which enemy of Batman's did he play in *Batman: Arkham City*?

_____

10. When he was offered the role of Batman, actor Val Kilmer was literally standing in a bat cave in Africa, having gone there to research a role for the film *The Ghost and the Darkness*.

○ **A.** True

○ **B.** False

11. In *Batman & Robin*, Batgirl's backstory was revised to make her Alfred's niece instead of Commissioner Gordon's daughter. Why?

○ **A.** Producers didn't want to bother explaining why she had never been seen in Gordon's company in the three previous films.

○ **B.** The screenwriter had been misinformed about Batgirl's history in the comics and honestly believed she was Alfred's niece.

○ **C.** It was thought that making her Alfred's niece would make her acceptance into the "Bat-Family" more believable.

○ **D.** It was believed that Pat Hingle, who played Commissioner Gordon, was too old to be believable as Batgirl's father.

12. In *Batman: Arkham City*, which of Batman's hated enemies forms a temporary alliance with him?

_____

13. In the videogame *Batman: Rise of Sin Tzu*, players could choose from four levels of difficulty. The levers were Easy, Medium, Hard, and . . .

_____

14. Kevin Conroy, known for the role of Bruce Wayne in *Batman: The Animated Series*, also played a character in the later cartoon show *The Batman*. Who was it?

_____

15. What Sega videogame from 1989 features an unauthorized appearance of Batman as a villain?

_____

16. Harley Quinn was supposed to die in a flashback scene in the animated film *Batman Beyond: Return of the Joker*, but her creator Paul Dini couldn't bring himself to do it. Instead, he snuck in another scene revealing that she had survived.

- ○ **A.** True
- ○ **B.** False

HARLEY QUINN!

Originally intended to be a throwaway character for one episode, Harley Quinn was a hugely popular creation of the team of *Batman: The Animated Series* and was later introduced into the official comic continuity. Creator Paul Dini has stated that he was inspired by seeing a TV show where Arleen Sorkin was dressed as a jester during a dream sequence. Arleen Sorkin, an old friend, was later cast to voice Harley Quinn herself.

17. In *Batman: The Brave and the Bold*, Katrina Moldoff was a thrill-seeker who adopted what costumed identity?

_____

18. In *Justice League Unlimited*, Peter MacNicol played a villain who caused quite a bit of trouble for time and space itself and was finally stopped by John Stewart and Batman. Who was he?

_____

19. In the videogame of *Batman: The Brave and the Bold*, what effect does Catman's gem have on humans?

_____

20. Initially, director Joel Schumacher was supposed to direct a follow-up sequel to the movie *Batman & Robin*. What was going to be the title of this fifth installment of the first Batman film franchise?

_____

21. Kevin Conroy played what mystical DC character in *Batman: The Brave and the Bold*?

_____

REUNION!

One of the most interesting reunions between Mark Hamill and Kevin Conroy occurred in an episode of *Batman: The Brave and the Bold*. In the story, Batman found the killer of his parents, and Hamill and Conroy appeared in the metaphorical roles of angel and demon. Conroy reminded the Dark Knight of his morality and devotion to justice while Hamill argued that vengeance demanded the killer's life as punishment for his own crimes.

22. In the live-action 1960s *Batman* series, where was the hidden switch that opened the secret entrance to the Batcave?

_____

23. In the cartoon *The Batman*, what was Mr. Freeze's chosen occupation before he was biologically altered and became a supervillain?

_____

24. The WB network would not allow Bruce Wayne's age to be revealed in *Batman Beyond* because they did not want kids to think Batman was old, even though he now had visible wrinkles and white hair, and walked with a cane.

○ **A.** True

○ **B.** False

25. In *Batman & Robin*, Batman pulls out a credit card. What is the comical expiration date on the card?

_____

26. In an episode of *Batman: The Brave and the Bold*, the Dark Knight was forced to temporarily adopt the identity of Batwoman.

○ **A.** True

○ **B.** False

27. In *Batman Forever*, when Dr. Chase Meridian visits Arkham Asylum, what is the name of the doctor who greets her?

_____

BURTON'S LETHAL BATMAN

Ever since 1940, DC Comics had followed a rule that Batman did not kill his enemies or believe in killing (though he was sympathetic to others who killed in self-defense). While killing occurred during true war on a battlefield, the Dark Knight felt his own war on crime did not justify slaughtering criminals who could be reformed. Despite this, Tim Burton's vision of Batman installed lethal weapons on the Batmobile, detonated bombs in buildings where he knew criminals were hiding, and trapped villains in lethal situations. All of this he apparently did without remorse, though in *Batman Forever*, Bruce Wayne expressed regret that vengeance had become his life (and then later killed Two-Face, despite this statement).

28. In the videogame *Batman: Arkham Asylum*, what villain is seen pacing but never reveals his true form?

_____

29. Originally, Rene Russo was supposed to play the role of Dr. Chase Meridian in *Batman Forever*. Soon after Michael Keaton decided not to return to the role of Batman, Rene Russo was replaced with Nicole Kidman. Why?

○ **A.** Rene Russo had only joined because of her friendship with Michael Keaton and wasn't terribly interested in continuing without him.

○ **B.** Rene Russo heard that Val Kilmer was going to be the new Batman and decided to leave due to an old grudge against him.

○ **C.** Rene Russo saw the script and thought it was too silly a story and not something she had interest in.

○ **D.** After Val Kilmer was cast as the new Batman, the filmmakers decided Rene Russo was too old to be his love interest, despite being only five years older.

30. In *Batman: The Brave and the Bold*, the Dark Knight journeyed to another world and met a counterpart dressed in a red and purple Batsuit. Who voiced the Batman of the planet Zur En Arrh?

_____

31. Christian Bale, who was twenty-one years old at the time, auditioned for the role of Robin in *Batman Forever*.

○ **A.** True

○ **B.** False

A NEW CRUSADE

Director Joel Schumacher wanted to bring a sense of lightheartedness to the Batman films and believed that the hero should "get over" the trauma of his parents' death. With Tim Burton as producer, *Batman Forever* saw Bruce Wayne facing his survivor's guilt and deciding that he would continue not because he *had* to be Batman but because he *chose* to be, an attitude the character had expressed in the comics many years before. This led way to an even more lighthearted take in Schumacher's next superhero film *Batman & Robin*.

32. In *Batman: The Movie* (1966), the Caped Crusader was attacked by a shark. What device was he lucky enough to have in his belt that was meant for just such a situation?

_____

33. Along with playing Batman, Rino Romano voiced a famous Marvel superhero in a TV series that only aired a few episodes in 1999. Who was it?

_____

34. What long-time love interest of Bruce Wayne's makes an appearance in *Batman: Arkham City*?

_____

35. The fifth movie in the Batman franchise that began with Burton's *Batman* was going to feature two villains joining forces against Batman, following the tradition begun in *Batman Returns*. Harley Quinn was going to be one villain. Who would have been her partner?

○ **A.** Mr. Zsasz

○ **B.** Owlman

○ **C.** Scarecrow

○ **D.** The Joker, with the explanation being that he had faked his death in Tim Burton's *Batman* film.

36. Julie Newmar made a special appearance in *Batman: The Brave and the Bold*. Whom did she play?

_____

37. What was the title of the show mentioned in Question 33?

_____

38. Though his voice is heard often in both games, the Riddler is never actually seen in *Batman: Arkham Asylum* or *Batman: Arkham City*.

○ **A.** True

○ **B.** False

PULLING BACK THE VIOLENCE

Batman: The Animated Series occasionally had to pull things back so the show would not be as dark as the comic. An episode in which Bruce attempted to escape a dream reality by potentially attempting suicide had to be softened. Batman seemed to reach most of the Joker's victims in time just before they died. And *Batman Beyond: Return of the Joker* had to alter scenes to lessen the amount of visible killing and violence (though a director's cut was later released). In contrast, *Batman: The Brave and the Bold* has impressed many by talking frankly about life and death, despite the fact that it is a youth-oriented show.

39. In *Batman: The Brave and the Bold*, the Caped Crusader joined forces with which hero against the villainous Sivana family?

40. In *The Batman*, Bruce Wayne's friend Ethan wound up becoming that show's version of what classic Batman enemy?

41. 1955's Miss America played Catwoman in *Batman: The Movie* (1966). Who is she?

42. In *Batman: The Brave and the Bold*, Green Arrow claims that the first time he met Batman, they fought against what sword-wielding villain?

43. This award-winning actor, singer, director, and magician has hosted the Emmy Awards, the Tony Awards, the Academy Awards, and the Spike TV Video Game Awards. He also lent his singing voice as the Music Meister in a musical episode of *Batman: The Brave and the Bold*. Who is he?

_____

44. Harvey Dent could not appear in the 2004 cartoon show *The Batman* due to a rights issue, since Warner Bros. was planning to feature him in the film *Batman Begins* and its sequel.

○ **A.** True

○ **B.** False

45. In *Batman: Arkham Asylum*, Jack Ryder reports on the trouble brewing at Arkham. Who is Ryder's superhero alter ego?

_____

46. In the 1989 *Batman* film, the Joker announces his plans to have a parade and explains where and when it will be. Despite the fact that they have been pursuing him for questioning in several deaths, the police are nowhere to be seen when the parade occurs and do not make any efforts to stop it. Why not?

○ **A.** The Joker had threatened the mayor of Gotham not to interfere.

○ **B.** The Joker had broadcast evidence indicating that he had been framed for the deaths.

○ **C.** Attorney Harvey Dent recommended taking no action, hoping to catch the Joker in the midst of a new crime rather than trying to connect him to strange deaths that might have been carried out by henchmen.

○ **D.** No explanation is given.

47. In the animated film *The Batman vs. Dracula*, what brilliant alias did the famous vampire use while pretending to be a cultural anthropologist?

48. When the Dark Knight and the Last Son of Krypton met in *The Batman Superman Movie: World's Finest*, Superman figured out that Batman and Bruce Wayne were the same person by matching their heartbeats with his super-hearing.

⚪ **A.** True

⚪ **B.** False

49. In *Batman Forever*, the scratches on Two-Face's coin are actually two letters. What are they?

SCHUMACHER'S BRUCE WAYNE — GOTHAM'S TONY STARK

In *Batman Forever*, director Joel Schumacher decided that, along with Batman getting over his trauma, the playboy disguise of Bruce Wayne should be dropped. Rather than pretending to be a lazy snob, Schumacher's Wayne was well known as an intelligent and charismatic man who personally oversaw his company's operations, displayed a keen understanding of advanced sciences, and would rush into danger even without a mask. Amazing how no one connected him with Batman.

50. Aquaman was a frequent guest star on *Batman: The Brave and the Bold*. What exclamation was he known for making in the heat of battle?

- ○ **A.** Fantastic!
- ○ **B.** Allons-y!
- ○ **C.** Fish-tastic!
- ○ **D.** Outrageous!

51. Which actor who once played Batman also played the role of Principal Kent Schwinger on *The Adventures of Pete & Pete* and voiced the retired Fearless Ferret on *Kim Possible*?

_____

52. In the "Emperor Joker" episode of *Batman: The Brave and the Bold*, the Joker repeatedly kills Batman and resurrects him with magic but never actually utters the word "death" or "kill" due to restrictions on the cartoon show.

- ○ **A.** True
- ○ **B.** False

53. Tom Kenny voices SpongeBob SquarePants. He also played what character in *The Batman* cartoon series?

_____

54. According to *Batman: The Brave and the Bold*, the hero Nightwing is deathly afraid of what animal?

- ○ **A.** Scorpions
- ○ **B.** Spiders
- ○ **C.** Monkeys
- ○ **D.** Spider monkeys

55. In the original proposal for the later-abandoned fifth installment of the first Batman film franchise, which would have followed *Batman & Robin*, what was Harley Quinn's backstory going to be?

- ○ **A.** She was a fan of the Joker who wanted revenge on Batman for the villain's death in the first film.
- ○ **B.** She was the Joker's daughter, who wanted revenge on Batman.
- ○ **C.** She was the Joker's sister, who believed her brother had not gone far enough and intended to outdo him.
- ○ **D.** She believed the Joker's spirit spoke to her and commanded her to take up his mission of chaos.

56. According to some accounts, what pop star was considered for the role of Harley Quinn in the film from Question 55?

_____

57. Before Mark Hamill joined the show, what famous actor was originally cast as the Joker for *Batman: The Animated Series* but was then let go because his performance was deemed too scary for the cartoon audience?

_____

THE INFLUENCE OF BATMAN'S ANIMATED ADVENTURES

Batman: The Animated Series stood out from other superhero cartoon adaptations. Scenes were animated on black boards to help develop the moody atmosphere. The opening theme footage displayed neither a title for the series nor the name of the character. Opening title cards were done in the style of Hitchcock, with a symbolic visual and a few moments of music to set the tone.

58. Billy Dee Williams was asked to reprise his role as Harvey Dent so he could then become Two-Face in the movie *Batman Forever*, but he refused unless he was given more screen time than Val Kilmer.

○ **A.** True

○ **B.** False

59. In the *Batman: The Brave and the Bold* episode "Legend of the Dark Mite," the magical Bat-Mite decides to give superpowers to what non-powered villain?

_____

60. The videogame *Batman: Arkham City* takes place how long after the events of *Batman: Arkham Asylum*?

_____

61. When Clark Kent and Bruce Wayne met in *The Batman Superman Movie: World's Finest*, the Gotham City hero remarked that he had been fighting crime for twelve years before the Man of Steel had shown up, noting he'd even had time to raise Dick Grayson for ten years and watch him recently evolve into Nightwing.

○ **A.** True

○ **B.** False

62. In Season 3, *Batman: The Animated Series* was retitled *The Adventures of Batman & Robin* and Fox insisted that they would not hear any new episode story pitches unless Robin played a key role. Why did Fox make this change in title and policy?

○ **A.** Fox wanted to emphasize the humor and lightheartedness of Robin because parents had brought up concerns that Batman's adventures were too dark.

○ **B.** Fox believed that most kids would not watch a TV show unless one of the main characters was also a kid.

○ **C.** Fox had decided that Season 3 would be the final season of the show and hoped that Robin would become popular enough to star in a spinoff series afterward.

○ **D.** Fox never has a reason for changing or canceling shows, it just acts at random.

63. John Glover played Jason Woodrue in *Batman & Robin*. Which other Batman villain did he play in *Batman: The Animated Series*?

_____

BURTON'S BRUCE WAYNE — A MYSTERY HIMSELF

While Bruce Wayne of the comics makes a show of being a bored playboy who may be intelligent but makes no effort to apply himself, Tim Burton's film version was a slightly socially awkward man who was notoriously reclusive, so much so that even local journalists were unaware what the billionaire looked like. In Burton's world, Wayne's life was very secretive and the murder of his parents was not a widely known historic event in Gotham City as it was in the comics. Somehow, the news media of Gotham did not connect this wealthy, traumatized recluse with the vigilante who used advanced weaponry and drove armored vehicles as he hunted criminals.

64. Which famous voice actor portrayed Harley Quinn in *Batman: Arkham City*?

_____

65. Name the episode of *Batman: The Brave and the Bold* where the Dark Knight uttered these lines: "I can't talk now. Skiing ninjas with lasers. Batman out!"

_____

66. The actor from Question 64 also played a Gotham City vigilante in *Batman: The Brave and the Bold*. Who was it?

_____

67. In the animated movie *The Batman vs. Dracula*, what long-time love interest of Bruce Wayne's made her cartoon debut?

_____

68. Adam West guest-starred as "Dr. Henry Wayne" on a live-action TV show in 1999 that featured one of Batman's inspirations. What was the show?

_____

69. In *Batman: Arkham City,* the Caped Crusader asks police officers for a codeword that Commissioner Gordon gave them. What is it?

_____

70. Debi Mazar and Drew Barrymore played Two-Face's aides in *Batman Forever*. What were their character names?

- ○ **A.** Yin and Yang
- ○ **B.** Dark and Light
- ○ **C.** Peace and Chaos
- ○ **D.** Sugar and Spice

71. Mark Hamill is normally associated with the Joker, but he also played a hero (albeit a dangerous one) in *Batman: The Brave and the Bold*. Can you guess who?

_____

72. Fox refused to hear a story pitch for *Batman: The Animated Series* for an episode where Catwoman would team up with the Black Canary. As a result, the latter was not introduced into DC animated continuity until several years later.

- ○ **A.** True
- ○ **B.** False

73. In the cartoon *The Batman*, what was Harley Quinn's profession before she became the Joker's accomplice?

_____

74. The Dave School produced a short animated film that featured Mark Hamill as the Joker but did not have Kevin Conroy voice Batman. Who played the Dark Knight instead?

_____

WHAT'S IN A VOICE?

After hearing more than 100 voice actors for the role of Batman, Kevin Conroy was chosen to voice the character in *Batman: TAS*. While many vocal performances were enjoyed on that show, many fans consider Conroy and Mark Hamill to be the definitive voices of Batman and the Joker. Many fan sites and blogs react with sadness and anger whenever an animated film for Batman is produced without the two actors reprising their famous roles.

75. What was the name of the Dave School short film?

_____

76. In *Batman: Arkham Asylum*, the body of what famous villain can be seen in Dr. Young's office?

_____

77. In the first story of *Superman: The Animated Series*, when Clark ponders beginning the life of a costumed hero, Ma Kent immediately comments that she doesn't want people to associate him with "that nut in Gotham City."

○ **A.** True

○ **B.** False

78. Unlike the comic books, the show *Batman Beyond* implies that Batgirl had a romantic affair at some point with whom?

_____

79. In *Batman: Arkham Asylum*, a special room exists where you can find plans and concept art for *Batman: Arkham City*.

○ **A.** True

○ **B.** False

80. In the cartoon series *The Batman*, Mark Hamill played neither a superhero nor a supervillain. Instead, he voiced a more down-to-earth criminal. Who was it?

_____

81. Along with playing Batman on another show, Will Friedle appeared in *The Batman* as a villain with technological enhancements. Which villain is that?

_____

82. In *Batman: The Animated Series*, Batman encountered his childhood hero the Grey Ghost. Who played this character?

_____

83. The *Batman: Arkham City* version of the Joker won Spike TV's 2011 Video Game Award for Best Character. A video was shown of the Joker accepting the award and then throwing away a script that he said he no longer needed. What was the title of the script?

_____

84. The short film from Question 74 also featured Dick Van Dyke. What role did he voice?

_____

85. In a proposed scene for the 1989 film *Batman*, Dick Grayson was going to appear in the story and wind up an orphan after the Joker killed his parents.

○ **A.** True

○ **B.** False

86. Jodi Benson played Aquagirl in *Batman Beyond*. What other cartoon aquatic character is she famous for playing?

_____

87. In *Batman: Arkham City*, Prof. Hugo Strange is voiced by Corey Burton. What heroic figure did he play on *Batman: The Brave and the Bold*?

_____

88. What 1960s cartoon superhero was a big inspiration in how animator Bruce Timm designed Batman's look for *Batman: The Animated Series*?

_____

89. The hero in Question 88 also appeared in what episode of *Batman: The Brave and the Bold*?

_____

90. During filming for *Batman Forever*, actor Chris O'Donnell accidentally damaged the Batmobile while driving it.

- ○ **A.** True
- ○ **B.** False

91. In the episode "Trails of the Demon!" in the series *Batman: The Brave and the Bold*, the demon Etrigan and Batman join forces with what legendary detective and army physician?

_____

92. In the upcoming cartoon show *Beware the Batman*, the Dark Knight will not be accompanied by Robin. What other costumed adventurer will be helping him in his adventures?

- ○ **A.** Black Lightning
- ○ **B.** Batgirl
- ○ **C.** Katana
- ○ **D.** Black Canary

THE DCAU

Many DC Comics fans refer to the mainstream universe of its superheroes as the DCU or DC Universe. Usually, different cartoon shows don't worry about continuity with each other, but the DC cartoons of the 1990s proved to be very different. *Superman: The Animated Series* clearly took place in the same reality as *Batman: TAS*. The shows *Batman Beyond* and *Justice League* expanded this continuity. Collectively, this became known as the DCAU (DC Animated Universe), and the term has been used to distinguish it from later cartoon shows and animated films that do not take place in this shared world.

93. To prepare for his role as the Joker, actor Heath Ledger read over a few Joker-centric comics, including the very first Joker story and what famous graphic novel illustrated by Brian Bolland?

_____

94. In the episode of *Batman: The Brave and the Bold* entitled "Legends of the Dark Mite," the pest known as Bat-Mite magically transforms the animated Batman into alternate versions of himself. Which of these were seen?

- ○ **A.** The *Batman Forever* version
- ○ **B.** The Adam West version
- ○ **C.** The *Dark Knight Returns* version
- ○ **D.** All of the above

CONNECTING THE DOTS

After *Batman Beyond* was canceled, the DCAU Bruce Wayne's activities could only be seen in the show *Justice League* and its successor *Justice League Unlimited*. The last episode of *JLU*, however, took place years after the events of *Batman Beyond*, providing a closing chapter to Batman, who had begun the DCAU, which was now coming to a close. Since then, DC superhero cartoons and animated films have usually been completely self-contained rather than connecting to others.

95. In *Batman: The Brave and the Bold*, who played Proto, the lovable bat-robot with the mind of a child?

_____

96. For what videogame did Morgan Freeman reprise the character of Lucius Fox?

_____

97. In *Batman: The Brave and the Bold*, what Christmas present did the Red Tornado give to the Dark Knight and what was written on it?

_____

98. This actor who became famous for his roles in westerns and for playing a dangerous cop was in consideration for the role of Two-Face in the 1960s *Batman* TV series. Name him.

_____

99. Though the character Two-Face never appeared on the show, the 1960s Batman TV series had an idea of introducing him as a news anchor whose face was scarred by an exploding camera.

○ **A.** True

○ **B.** False

100. Which famous radio vigilante got a short-lived live-action TV show due to the success of the 1960s Batman series?

_____

101. Which martial arts star first rose to fame thanks to the TV show featuring the character mentioned in Question 100?

_____

102. Characters such as Black Vulcan, Apache Chief, Samurai, and the Wonder Twins were created for the *Super Friends* cartoon shows. These characters appeared again, with new names and costumes, in an episode of *Justice League Unlimited*. What were they collectively called in *JLU*?

_____

103. Although it became widely known to TV audiences, the Hall of Justice building that first appeared on the *Super Friends* cartoon show never made it into the official comic book stories of the Justice League.

○ **A.** True

○ **B.** False

104. Due to a rights issue, a young Bruce Wayne was not allowed to appear on the TV series *Smallville*. Which superhero filled his role as a powerless vigilante who became close friends with Clark Kent despite their different attitudes on justice?

_____

105. In the first episode of *Young Justice*, what secret agency did Robin, Aqualad, and Kid Flash cross swords with?

_____

106. Based on evidence from a visit to the future and his own memories, which version of Robin starred in the cartoon show *Teen Titans*? Dick Grayson, Jason Todd, Tim Drake, or Damian Wayne?

_____

107. In the comics, Jason Todd's resurrection was said to be the result of cosmic forces unleashed by the character Superboy-Prime. In the animated film *Batman: Under the Red Hood*, who was responsible for Jason Todd coming back from the dead?

_____

108. Since the *Teen Titans* cartoon show was aimed at younger viewers, what was the assassin Deathstroke exclusively called whenever he showed up?

_____

109. Though Robin is usually the natural leader of the Teen Titans and Young Justice teams in the comics, the show *Young Justice* places who as the team's original leader?

_____

110. Efrem Zimbalist Jr. played Dr. Octopus in *Spider-Man: The Animated Series* on Fox and Zorro's father, Don Alejandro, in the live-action *Zorro* series. Whom did he play on *Batman: The Animated Series* and *Justice League*?

_____

111. Due to a rights issue, once *The Batman* began airing on WB, Cartoon Network did not use any of Batman's villains or related cast members (such as Nightwing, Robin, etc.) for the rest of the *Justice League Unlimited* cartoon series.

○ **A.** True

○ **B.** False

112. Which star of *Law & Order* and the movie *Clueless* voiced Batman in the animated film *Justice League: The New Frontier*?

_____

113. The popular story *JLA: Tower of Babel* involved a villain stealing weapons Batman had designed to take down his Justice League teammates in case they went rogue. What animated film adapted this story?

_____

114. In the animated film *Justice League: Crisis on Two Earths*, the roles of Batman and his evil counterpart Owlman were played by the same actor.

○ **A.** True

○ **B.** False.

115. In *Batman: The Brave and the Bold*, Batman and the Batman of Zur En Arrh joined forces against a villain who bore a resemblance to Lex Luthor. What was his name?

_____

116. A pitch for a live-action series that would depict a young Bruce Wayne and his journey to become Batman, with Harvey Dent as a friend fated to become an enemy, failed to generate interest. The creators then changed the pitch and wound up producing what long-running TV show instead?

_____

117. FoxTeca was a company mentioned in episodes of *Batman Beyond*. Who started this company?

_____

118. In the two-part story "The Once and Future Thing" on *Justice League Unlimited*, what strange image did John Stewart and Batman see before reality was restored?

_____

119. Terry McGinnis wore a high-tech Batsuit in *Batman Beyond*. This suit is downloadable content for which Batman videogame?

_____

120. In *Batman Beyond*, a group of heroes appeared who were an homage to Marvel's Fantastic Four. What were they called?

_____

121. Which alien enemy did Terry and the Justice League Unlimited team of the future join forces against in a two-part story in *Batman Beyond*?

_____

122. Aside from *Batman: The Rise of Sin-Tzu*, which videogame was done in the style of *Batman: The Animated Series*?

_____

123. When *Batman: The Animated Series* evolved into *The New Batman Adventures*, there was a rule that each episode had to have a supervillain. Previously episodes could focus on realistic, human criminals and gangsters as well.

○ **A.** True

○ **B.** False

124. The villain of the animated film *Batman: Mask of the Phantasm* was inspired by what character from the comic book story *Batman: Year Two*?

_____

125. *Batman Beyond* had a spinoff show that did not involve any DC Comics superheroes. What was it titled?

_____

126. Which actor, who was also featured in *Batman: The Brave and the Bold*, played the titular character of the show mentioned in Question 125?

_____

127. With the exception of Batman and Robin's origins, Fox insisted that all episodes of *Batman: The Animated Series* be original stories rather than adaptations of published comic books.

○ **A.** True

○ **B.** False

128. Like his mentor, Terry McGinnis eventually fell for a criminal. What criminal alias did she use?

_____

129. What group did the woman from Question 128 belong to?

_____

130. Which episode of *Batman: The Animated Series* won the 1993 Emmy for Most Outstanding Writing in an Animated Program?

_____

131. What is the name of the mercenary group that Strange hires in *Batman: Arkham City*?

_____

132. Although he was later asked to reprise the Joker in what would have been the fifth movie of the first Batman film franchise, Jack Nicholson declined because he did not like stories that resurrected dead characters.

○ **A.** True

○ **B.** False

133. Believing his performance in *Batman: Arkham Asylum* ended the Joker on a high note, Mark Hamill was reluctant to return as the Clown Prince of Killers for *Batman: Arkham City*. What made him change his mind?

_____

134. Which episode of *Batman: The Animated Series* won the 1993 Emmy for Most Outstanding Half Hour or Less Program?

_____

135. *Batman: The Animated Series* created a new origin for Mr. Freeze that became so popular, it was later adapted as his origin into the comics.

○ **A.** True

○ **B.** False

Chapter 6 Answer Key

1. The library had a hidden access to the bat-poles.
2. C.
3. The bottom of a beer or soda bottle.
4. A-iv, B-vi, C-v, D-ii, E-i, F-iii
5. Black Mask.
6. Pottery.
7. False.
8. B.
9. The Mad Hatter.
10. True.
11. D.
12. Bane.
13. Dark Knight.
14. Dick Grayson's father.
15. *The Revenge of Shinobi.*
16. True.
17. Batwoman.
18. Chronos.
19. It turns people into kitties.
20. *Batman Triumphant.*
21. The Phantom Stranger.
22. Inside a bust of Shakespeare.
23. A professional thief.
24. True.
25. "Forever."
26. True. He had switched bodies with Batwoman.
27. Dr. Burton.
28. Clayface.
29. D.
30. Kevin Conroy.
31. True.
32. Bat-Shark Repellent.
33. Spider-Man.
34. Vicki Vale.
35. C, although there was talk of having the Joker appear during gas-induced hallucinations.
36. Martha Wayne.
37. *Spider-Man Unlimited.*
38. False, he's only visibly absent during *Arkham Aslyum.*
39. Captain Marvel (Shazam is also an acceptable answer).
40. Clayface.
41. Lee Meriwether.
42. The Cavalier.
43. Neil Patrick Harris.
44. True.
45. The Creeper.
46. D.
47. Dr. Alucard (Dracula spelled backwards).
48. False.
49. His initials, H.D.
50. D.
51. Adam West.
52. False, he uses those words freely.
53. The Penguin.
54. C.
55. B.
56. Madonna.
57. Tim Curry.
58. False. He very much wanted to return to the role but was bought out.
59. Calendar Man.

60. 18 months later.

61. False, although based on the timeline of *Batman: The Animated Series*, that assessment would likely be accurate.

62. B.

63. Riddler.

64. Tara Strong.

65. "Crisis at 22,300 Miles!"

66. Huntress.

67. Vicki Vale.

68. *Zorro.*

69. "Sarah."

70. D.

71. The Spectre.

72. True.

73. She hosted a pop psychology talk show.

74. Adam West.

75. *Batman: New Times.*

76. Ra's al Ghul.

77. True.

78. Batman.

79. True.

80. Tony Zucco.

81. Gearhead.

82. Adam West.

83. *Arkham World.*

84. Commissioner Gordon.

85. True.

86. Ariel from *The Little Mermaid.*

87. Red Tornado.

88. Space Ghost.

89. "Bold Beginnings."

90. True.

91. Sherlock Holmes and Dr. Watson.

92. C.

93. *Batman: The Killing Joke.*

94. D.

95. Adam West.

96. The *Batman Begins* videogame.

97. A coffee mug with the words "World's Greatest Detective."

98. Clint Eastwood.

99. True.

100. The Green Hornet.

101. Bruce Lee, who played Kato.

102. The Ultimen.

103. False.

104. Oliver Queen, Green Arrow.

105. The Cadmus Project.

106. Dick Grayson.

107. Ra's al Ghul.

108. Slade.

109. Aqualad.

110. Alfred Pennyworth.

111. True.

112. Jeremy Sisto.

113. *Justice League: Doom.*

114. False.

115. Rohtul.

116. *Smallville.*

117. Lucius Fox.

118. A giant hand holding a cluster of stars.

119. *Batman: Arkham City.*

120. Terrific Trio.

121. Starro the Conqueror (the Star Conqueror also works as an answer).

122. *Batman: Vengeance.*

123. True.

124. The Reaper.

125. *The Zeta Project.*

126. Diedrich Bader.

127. False. Many episodes were indeed directly based on comic book stories.

128. Ten.

129. The Royal Flush Gang.

130. "Heart of Ice."

131. TYGER Security.

132. False. Jack Nicholson actually expressed great interest in the character being resurrected somehow so he could return.

133. The involvement of Kevin Conroy and Paul Dini.

134. "Robin's Reckoning."

135. True.

Score Your Bat-Knowledge!

In this section, there are 140 possible right answers.

If you got 1–67 right, then you may have a surface knowledge, but you could stand to delve deeper.

If you got 68–104 right, you're familiar with a few games, shows, and films you've enjoyed, but don't act like you're an expert to your friends just yet.

If you got 105–140 right, congratulations! You are truly a connoisseur of Batman adaptations!

CHAPTER 7

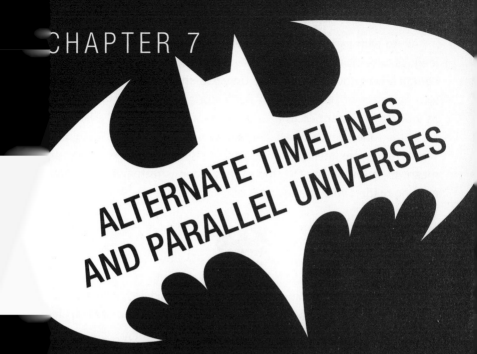

ALTERNATE TIMELINES AND PARALLEL UNIVERSES

D C Comics is almost synonymous with the word "multiverse." The ball started rolling with the introduction of Earth-2. Writers and artists realized that by having an alternate reality, you could do whatever you wanted to with parallel world counterparts of heroes like Batman because it would have no real consequence on the main titles. Since Batman is one of DC's most popular and marketable characters, major changes to Bruce Wayne's life must be carefully considered and plotted out. But if you're talking about the older Batman of Earth-2, then there's instantly more freedom.

Along with Earth-2, a well-known parallel reality of DC Comics is Earth-3, where alternate versions of Batman and his allies are villains instead of heroes. Later on, a similar mirror Earth was discovered in a parallel anti-matter universe that had often been visited by the Green Lantern Corps. On both Earth-3 and the Anti-Matter Earth, Batman's counterpart was known as the Owlman, a member of the Crime Syndicate.

Along with various other parallel worlds that Batman and his colleagues have visited, DC Comics has published several stories that are completely removed from the DC Universe, shifting familiar characters into new sets of circumstances. Such stories might imagine Batman as a pirate or Superman as a knight or Wonder Woman as a law officer of the American Old West. These tales used to be called "imaginary stories" and were later given the label of Elseworlds in 1991. They are meant to make familiar DC characters suddenly fresh and new again, exciting readers with strange possibilities.

1. *Batman: Gotham by Gaslight* is generally considered to be the first Elseworlds story. In it, which notorious figure came to Gotham City and clashed with Batman?

_____

2. On Earth-2, an older Bruce Wayne eventually retired from his activities as Batman. After years of philanthropy and civic volunteerism, the retirement of a major figure in Gotham City led to Bruce assuming what new job?

_____

3. In the cartoon *Batman: The Brave and the Bold* Batman encountered a world similar to Earth-3 and the anti-matter Earth. On this planet, what criminal gang had defeated nearly all of the local heroes?

_____

4. Earth-10 is a reality where the Axis Powers won World War II. On this Earth, the Justice League Axis has its own version of Batman. What is he called?

_____

5. In the story *Batman: In Darkest Knight*, Bruce Wayne is pondering the best way to begin his war on crime when he encounters a dying alien named Abin Sur. What object does Abin give Bruce Wayne?

_____

6. Regarding the alternate Earth mentioned in Question 3, what was the name of the hero who reached out to Batman for aid?

_____

7. In the alternate reality of the *Thrillkiller* graphic novels, Bruce Wayne only becomes Batman after the death of which hero?

_____

8. On Earth-5, an elderly version of Bruce Wayne served as an ally to Captain Marvel.

○ **A.** True

○ **B.** False

9. In the Amalgam Universe, story elements and characters from Marvel and DC Comics were combined. The character Dark Claw was a fusion of Batman and which Marvel superhero?

_____

10. In *Batman: Castle of the Bat*, Bruce Wayne resurrects his father, turning him into a monstrous Bat-Man in the process. This story is loosely based on what classic novel that has inspired many comics and films?

_____

11. In *Batman: Brotherhood of the Bat* (1995), readers see a world fifty years into the future. Batman is long dead and in his place stands an order of assassins who are all dressed in an alternate version of the Batsuit. Who created this organization?

_____

12. What was the title of the first comic to feature the Elseworlds logo on its cover?

_____

13. In his early appearances, the Earth-3 version of the villain Owlman had limited mind-control abilities, even though his counterpart Batman is famous for having no powers.

○ **A.** True

○ **B.** False

WHO IS THE OWLMAN?

On the anti-matter Earth, Owlman is a counterpart to Batman but is not literally an evil Bruce Wayne. In his reality, the Waynes had two children, Bruce and the elder Thomas Jr. When Thomas Wayne Sr. refused to be brought in for questioning by the GCPD, violence ensued, resulting in the deaths of his wife Martha and young Bruce. Thomas Jr. saw this and blamed his father. Fleeing the scene, the boy was raised by a criminal and dedicated his life to acquiring power and defeating, as well as humiliating, the forces of law and order on his planet. With drugs to enhance his brain power, he is the tactical genius of the Crime Syndicate of Amerika, a group that unofficially rules much of the anti-matter Earth through fear.

14. On Earth-2, Alfred did not join Wayne Manor until after Batman and Robin had already begun their crime-fighting careers.

○ **A.** True

○ **B.** False

15. In the DC multiverse, Earth-9 features the world of the Tangent comics line. In this reality, the Batman was originally a knight named Sir William. What legendary witch attempted to manipulate him to commit murder?

_____

16. Regarding Question 15, whom was Sir William meant to kill?

_____

17. In *Superman: Speeding Bullets*, Kal-El of Krypton was found and adopted by the Wayne family, as Thomas and Martha did not have a child of their own. In this story, moments after the Waynes were murdered, what happened to their killer Joe Chill?

---

18. *Batman Annual* #18 featured a version of Batman who studied under Leonardo da Vinci. What large piece of equipment did this alternate Dark Knight use to fight evil?

---

19. In the miniseries *JSA: The Liberty Files*, Bruce Wayne operated as a spy for the United States, known as the Bat. In what era did this story take place?

HOME-FIELD ADVANTAGE

In *JLA: Earth 2*, the Justice League thought they could save the Earth of the anti-matter universe and set things right. But this is a world that was meant to be the opposite of the DC Universe Earth. And in the DCU, good tends to win out over evil, no matter what the odds. Therefore, despite their best efforts, the League realized that this was a reality where good could never fully take hold. The Crime Syndicate of Amerika was as much a reflection of that as anything else.

20. In the story *Superman: Speeding Bullets*, an alternate version of Lex Luthor suffered facial disfiguration and then adopted a new criminal alias. What was it?

_____

21. What is the title of the graphic novel that served as a sequel to *Batman: Gotham by Gaslight*?

_____

22. On Earth-2, how old was Dick Grayson when he was taken in by Bruce Wayne?

○ **A.** 8

○ **B.** 10

○ **C.** 12

○ **D.** 14

23. On Earth-2, Batman finally let his guard down and admitted his love for Catwoman when the two were working against one of Gotham's notorious villains. Which criminal was this?

_____

24. On Earth-9, the Tangent version of Batman is a knight under a spell. What is the nature of this spell?

○ **A.** He will remain in Castle Bat until he redeems himself with good deeds, performing them by having his spirit inhabit a suit of armor outside of the castle.

○ **B.** His body remains in a coma in Castle Bat while his soul is trapped inside a suit of armor, unable to find release until he finishes 2000 years of heroic service to the Earth.

○ **C.** His form has been mutated into that of a bat, and he will not become human again until he has done enough good in the world.

○ **D.** He is trapped in his armor, unable to remove it without feeling intense pain, until he is forgiven by those souls he unjustly killed.

25. In his normal stories, Rex Tyler was the superhero called Hourman. What was his code name in *JSA: The Liberty Files*?

_____

26. In *Batman/Captain America*, readers saw a world where Batman and Cap both operated during the 1940s. What two villains were featured in this story?

_____

BATMAN JR. AND ROBIN SR.

In a couple of imaginary stories, Alfred wrote his own form of fan fiction, describing a future in which Batman settled down and had a son, Bruce Jr. Following Bruce's retirement Dick Grayson, all grown up, would become the new Batman and Bruce Jr. would eventually join him as the new Robin. Decades later, in the pages of *JLA*, writer Grant Morrison returned to this idea when Bruce Wayne had a dream of a similar future. Nine years after that, Morrison made it reality by introducing Damian Wayne, Bruce's son by Talia, in 2008, connecting it to a 1987 story (that had been considered out of continuity for years) where readers saw that the Dark Knight had fathered a child. Damian then became Robin a year later when the adult Dick Grayson temporarily assumed the guise of Batman.

27. When Batman retired on Earth-2, Dick Grayson continued protecting Gotham City. What new identity did he assume?

- ○ **A.** Batman
- ○ **B.** Nightwing
- ○ **C.** Red Robin
- ○ **D.** He still used the name Robin but now wore different costumes.

28. In what story did readers see a futuristic world where people worshipped a god called "the Bruce"?

29. In his final adventure, after years of being retired, the Batman of Earth-2 took up his cape and cowl again to protect Gotham City from a mystically empowered villain. What was the name of this criminal?

30. When Marvel Comics creator Stan Lee gave his own take on Robin, whom did he say had raised the teen to be a thief and a killer?

_____

31. On Earth-2, Selina Kyle only married Bruce Wayne after she had voluntarily served prison time for her crimes as Catwoman.

○ **A.** True

○ **B.** False

32. One difference between the mainstream Batman and the Batman of Earth-2 was that the latter had a personal vice that later endangered his health. What was it?

_____

33. The cartoon *Batman: The Brave and the Bold* featured the Blue Bowman, an evil version of Green Arrow from a parallel Earth. In the comics, "Blue Bowman" was an alias temporarily used by a known Batman enemy. Who was it?

○ **A.** Signalman

○ **B.** Merlyn the Archer

○ **C.** Kite-Man

○ **D.** The Celestial Toymaker

34. On Earth-2, Helena Wayne worked with many heroes but she was especially close to a blonde dressed in red, white, and blue. Who was this other hero?

_____

35. In *The Dark Knight Returns*, Green Arrow was sporting a noticeable injury. What was it?

_____

36. In the pages of *Kingdom Come*, readers met a young man named Ibn al Xu'ffasch, the heir to Ra's al Ghul's empire. What is the English translation of this young man's name?

_____

37. The person in Question 34 originally called what place home?

_____

38. In the Amalgam Universe, the hero Dark Claw's real name was Logan Wayne. A man named Bruce Wayne also inhabited this universe. What organization did Bruce belong to?

_____

39. In the Tangent reality of Earth-9, the "Joker" was an identity shared by three women. One was named Christy Xanadu. Who were the other two?

_____

40. In *JSA: The Liberty Files*, the Owl was a counterpart to what DC Comics superhero?

_____

CRACKED MIRROR

On the surface, the Owlman of the anti-matter Earth seems much like Batman, despite the different costume and lethal tactics. Yet there's more to it than that. As Batman has explained, he respects fear but does not enjoy it. This is a crusade for him, one he knows he can't win but where he can at least make a difference, and he focuses on pragmatism rather than being sensitive to the feelings of his allies. On the other hand, Owlman sees no reason why he can't have all he desires and he delights in making others afraid or uncomfortable, knowing just what to say to make their egos crack. And while Batman does everything he can to stop criminal operations, Owlman sometimes funds his own opposition to ensure there are always new opponents and challenges.

41. On Earth-2, after the death of Batman, what did the heroic sorcerer Dr. Fate do as one last favor for his fallen comrade?

 ○ **A.** He caused a giant statue of Batman to materialize in the center of Gotham Square.

 ○ **B.** He eliminated the general public's memory of the revelation of Batman's identity, protecting the secret identities of Dick Grayson and Helena Wayne.

 ○ **C.** He caused Wayne Manor to collapse into the Batcave, ensuring no criminals would be able to ransack the place and use Batman's technology and secrets for their own gain.

 ○ **D.** He traveled back in time and told a younger Bruce Wayne that his life would have meaning.

42. As seen in the episode "Mite-fall!" of *Batman: The Brave and the Bold*, the Dark Knight once traveled to a parallel dimension and saved what famous historical figure from assassination?

43. What was the name of the technologically enhanced villain featured in the episode from Question 42?

_____

44. Helena Wayne of Earth-2 had a superpowered best friend. Who was the Earth-1 counterpart of this person?

_____

45. Helena Wayne's first appearance outside of comics was in what NBC TV special?

_____

46. Why does Owlman search for Earth-Prime in _Justice League: Crisis on Two Earths_?

_____

47. Who was the Earth-1 counterpart of Helena Wayne's friend from Question 34?

_____

CAMEOS GALORE

Batman is so popular in mainstream comics and as an Elseworlds veteran that he'll show up in alternate realities even when it's not his story. In one tale of an Earth that was conquered by Krypton, Batman is a gruff, old rebel, constantly showing the Kryptonians that humanity cannot be controlled. He meets young Kal-El and his words, along with his death, inspire the Kryptonian to take up arms against his own people and free the Earth under the name "Superman."

48. What health condition was already threatening the life of Earth-2's Bruce Wayne when he was killed?

49. In *Legends of the Dark Knight Annual* #4, an Elseworlds story entitled "Citizen Wayne" showed a world where Bruce did not become Batman. Who took on that costumed identity instead?

50. In the Amalgam Universe, Dark Claw's greatest enemy was Creed H. Quinn. What alias did this villain use?

51. In the Amalgam Universe, Dark Claw's ally Sparrow was a fusion of Robin and which Marvel hero?

52. After witnessing the deaths of his mother and younger brother, Thomas Wayne Jr. fled the scene and was raised by a criminal whom he considered a hero. Who raised the boy who would become the Owlman of the anti-matter Earth?

53. Which MIT dropout who then went into acting wound up playing the voice of Owlman in the film *Justice League: Crisis on Two Earths*?

54. Which actor, normally known for comedy, voiced a different universe's Owlman in *Batman: The Brave and the Bold*?

_____

55. Owlman is often entangled in an affair with Superwoman. Who is her counterpart in the mainstream DC Universe?

_____

IT'S ALL IN FUN!

Some Elseworlds stories may seem silly. But if you think about it, they're all silly. Batman as a vampire? Batman during the Civil War, wearing blue and gray? It's all in good fun. Writers and artists enjoy the freedom of not holding back on ideas, however bizarre they may be, and fans have often enjoyed and chuckled at the little jokes that occur. For instance, in *Batman: The Brave and the Bold*, the Batman of Zur En Arrh was raised and assisted by a robot butler named . . . Alpha-Red!

56. The Crime Syndicate of Amerika is not the only great evil in the anti-matter universe. In the same universe what planet is known as a den of evil and violence?

_____

57. The Batman has Robin as his squire. On Earth-3, what was the name of Owlman's young, violent partner?

_____

58. When Stan Lee of Marvel Comics reimagined Batman, he said that his name was Wayne Williams. What profession did Williams have that involved wearing a costume and calling himself Batman?

_____

59. In *Batman: Holy Terror*, who gives his life to save Batman from an evil witch?

_____

60. In a couple of stories, readers meet Leatherwing, a Batman who served as a pirate of sorts on the high seas. Who employed Leatherwing?

_____

61. What was the name of Captain Leatherwing's fine ship?

_____

62. In Captain Leatherwing's world, who was the madman who traveled on the ship *Pescador*?

_____

63. Captain Leatherwing met an enticing woman who commanded the *Cat's Paw*. Name this captain.

_____

64. What was the first book of the Elseworlds Batman Vampire trilogy?

○ **A.** *Batman vs. Dracula*

○ **B.** *Batman and Dracula: Lord of Vampires*

○ **C.** *Batman and Dracula: Red Rain*

○ **D.** *Batman: Red Rain*

65. In another Elseworlds story, Batman joined forces with a Jewish magician to fight vampires. Who was this magician?

_____

66. In the Elseworlds Batman Vampire trilogy, Batman painted a cross at one point to ward off Dracula. What did he use to paint the cross?

_____

67. In 1990, DC Comics published *Batman: Digital Justice* by Pepe Moreno. What out-of-the-ordinary feature concerning the comic's art was advertised on the cover?

_____

68. Who becomes Batman in *Batman: Digital Justice,* and how is he related to one of Bruce Wayne's allies?

_____

KINGDOM COME

One of the most famous Elseworlds stories is *Kingdom Come*, produced by Mark Waid and Alex Ross. Though on the surface it's another "dark, possible future" tale where the old guard returns to set things right, there's also another layer. The story is a criticism of the antiheroes and lethal vigilantes who had come into prominence in the late 1980s and early 1990s, bringing with them an attitude that emulated that of *Watchmen* and *The Dark Knight Returns*. As Waid and Ross show in *Kingdom Come*, these attitudes are not altruistic enough or focused enough and the result is that the battles become less about good and evil and more akin to rival gangs arguing over whose philosophy is better. Which is when you need to bring back Superman . . .

69. In *Kingdom Come*, an older Batman used an exoskeleton to help maintain the body he'd put so much stress on in his younger years. This exoskeleton was based on the armor of which movie character?

_____

70. In *Batman: Brotherhood of the Bat*, Bruce Wayne has a son by Talia but he is not named Damian. What is his name?

_____

71. What was the name of the popular superhero restaurant chain in *Kingdom Come*?

_____

72. Look at the epilogue to *Kingdom Come* closely. What popular non-superpower-endowed DC character seems to have his stuffed body on display?

_____

73. In 2006, Paul Pope produced an Elseworlds miniseries that featured a futuristic Batman but did not carry the Elseworlds label. What was its title?

_____

74. In *Kingdom Come*, Dick Grayson returned to the life of a superhero after years of retirement but did not resume his Nightwing identity. What was he called?

_____

75. In one Elseworlds story, Bruce Wayne joined the Secret Society of Detectives, formed by Alan Pinkerton. What was Bruce's code name and the title of this book?

_____

76. In the Elseworlds story *JLA: Act of God*, what happened to Earth's superhumans that resulted in Batman training a new team?

_____

FAMILY REUNION!

A few times, the different Batmen from many Elseworlds stories have met. In *Countdown Arena*, different versions of Bruce Wayne were forced to fight by the villain Monarch. Later on, the same story had different versions of Earth's Green Lanterns fight each other, including one who was really Bruce Wayne! And in the episode "Game Over for Owlman" in *Batman: The Brave and the Bold*, the Dark Knight recruited several versions of himself from across reality (one of whom was a vampire) to help him thwart Owlman's schemes.

77. Match the villain from *Justice League: Crisis on Two Earths* with their heroic counterpart from the mainstream DC Universe.

___ **A.** Aurora	**i.** Looker
___ **B.** Scream Queen	**ii.** Vibe
___ **C.** Sai	**iii.** Black Lightning
___ **D.** Breakdance	**iv.** Halo
___ **E.** Model Citizen	**v.** Katana
___ **F.** Black Power	**vi.** Black Canary

Chapter 7 Answer Key

1. Jack the Ripper.

2. Police commissioner.

3. Injustice Syndicate.

4. Leatherwing.

5. A Green Lantern power ring.

6. The Red Hood.

7. Robin.

8. False.

9. Wolverine.

10. Frankenstein.

11. Ra's al Ghul.

12. *Batman: Holy Terror.*

13. True.

14. True.

15. Morgan le Fay

16. King Arthur.

17. Kal burned his face away with heat-vision.

18. Leonardo's hang glider.

19. The 1940s, during World War II.

20. The Joker.

21. *Batman: Master of the Future.*

22. A.

23. Scarecrow.

24. A.

25. The Clock.

26. Red Skull and the Joker.

27. D.

28. *I, Joker.*

29. Jensen.

30. Reverend Darkk.

31. True.

32. Smoking a pipe.

33. A.

34. Power Girl.

35. He was missing an arm.

36. Son of the Bat.

37. Krypton.

38. S.H.I.E.L.D.

39. Lori Lemaris and Mary Marvel.

40. Hourman.

41. B.

42. Abraham Lincoln.

43. John Wilkes Boom.

44. Huntress.

45. *Legend of the Super-Heroes.*

46. He thinks destroying it, and the multiverse, will be the only original act he will ever do.

47. Supergirl.

48. Cancer.

49. Harvey Dent.

50. Hyena.

51. Jubilee.

52. Joe Chill.

53. James Woods.

54. Diedrich Bader.

55. Wonder Woman.

56. Qward.

57. Talon.

58. Professional wrestler.

59. Barry Allen.

60. The British Crown (specifically, King James).

61. The *Flying Fox.*

62. The Laughing Man.

63. Capitana Felina.

64. C.

65. Harry Houdini.

66. His own blood.

67. It was completely computer generated.

68. Det. James Gordon, grandson of Commissioner Jim Gordon.

69. Darth Vader.

70. Talon.

71. Planet Krypton.

72. Jonah Hex.

73. *Batman: Year 100.*

74. Red Robin.

75. *Detective # 27.*

76. They all lost their powers one day.

77. A-iv, B-vi, C-v, D-ii, E-i, F-iii.

Score Your Bat-Knowledge!

In this section, there are 82 possible right answers.

If you got 0–36 right, then you've barely ventured out beyond the familiar mainstream reality and it shows.

If you got 37–60 right, you've checked out some of the alternate universes, but you need to go beyond the obvious ones most people talk about and look up some other stories that may surprise you.

If you got 61–82 right, congratulations! You are a true explorer of the multiverse!

CHAPTER 8

THE CREATORS

*I*t's different with a book series. A character can be around for years and yet only have a handful of novels to his or her name, each penned by the same author, who decided on the direction and where the story had to end. Mainstream comics operate by a different set of rules when it comes to superheroes. Writers come and go, artists may leave in the middle of a story, editors can shift and request entirely new directions at the drop of a hat.

Though Batman may have been initially created by Bob Kane and Bill Finger, it would be a mistake to say that their version was the end-all and be-all. Since 1939, Batman has been added to by hundreds of writers and even more artists, his character evolving and changing under different influences. Some ideas get abandoned. Some change in the process of writing. Some writers wind up revising the past and/or recycling story elements they used with other characters. Take a peek behind the curtain and learn more about who was literally at the drawing board and who was guiding the stories.

1. When Bob Kane first designed Batman, he thought the hero's bodysuit should be what color?

○ **A.** Gray

○ **B.** Black

○ **C.** Blue

○ **D.** Red

2. The very first intercompany superhero crossover, featuring a Marvel hero meeting a DC hero, included art by what influential Batman artist?

_____

3. What was the title of the crossover book mentioned in Question 2?

_____

4. Who was the longtime Batman writer who considered himself an anarchist and created the character Anarky to express his ideas?

_____

5. With artist Neal Adams, writer Dennis O'Neil (who would later become editor of the Batman titles) wrote a story for *Batman* #251 (1973) that brought the Joker back after an absence of several years and returned him to his mass-murdering roots. What was the title of this now-famous story?

_____

6. Alan Brennert has written several acclaimed stories featuring Batman and also wrote several scripts for the live-action *Wonder Woman* TV series of the 1970s. For what legal drama did he win an Emmy Award as a producer and writer?

_____

7. What famous Batman writer began his career with the creation of a character named Gideon Stargrave?

_____

8. What longtime Batman writer also created the Marvel character Moon Knight, who has often been compared to Batman?

_____

9. In Batman's very first comic book story, Alfred was depicted as a fat, clean-shaven man rather than a thin man with a mustache.

○ **A.** True

○ **B.** False

BILL FINGER—THE OTHER CREATOR

By his own admission, Bob Kane enjoyed coming up with ideas for characters but wasn't terribly talented in scripting them out or developing a backstory. Kane met writer Bill Finger at a party and offered him a job as a ghost writer. If not for Finger, many elements of what readers consider today to be essential to the Batman mythos would not exist. By Kane's own words, he had envisioned Batman with a noticeably different look and as a straightforward vigilante. It was Finger who gave the hero his real name, origin story, and demonic appearance, altering the character into a driven "scientific detective."

10. Sketches by what famous artist inspired the idea of Batman's winged cloak?

_____

11. Houghton, Michigan's newspaper *The Daily Mining Gazette* profiled this man in 1976 as a "near-master cartoonist." Who is he?

_____

12. In 1978, Dennis O'Neil and Neal Adams presented a special oversized comic featuring Superman fighting what famous sports figure?

_____

13. Bob Kane's early ideas for Batman were inspired by *The Bat Whispers* and which other film?

○ **A.** *The Scarlet Pimpernel*

○ **B.** *The Mark of Zorro*

○ **C.** *The Man Who Laughs*

○ **D.** A & B

14. Bill Finger suggested that Batman's mask give him blank eyes. What previously existing masked hero inspired this design choice?

_____

ORIGIN OF THE COWL

In Bob Kane's initial design, Batman wore a simple domino mask that covered his eyes, similar to the mask later worn by Robin. Bill Finger then suggested having the winged cape attached to a horned cowl, mimicking a bat's ears while also giving Batman a more menacing appearance.

15. Bob Kane's original design for Batman involved exposed hands.

- ○ **A.** True
- ○ **B.** False

16. In an issue of *The Batman Adventures*, based on *Batman: The Animated Series*, three DC Comics editors were portrayed as super-villains. Mr. Nice was based on Archie Goodwin. Who were the inspirations for the characters known as Mastermind and the Perfesser?

_____

17. Bill Finger was the one to come up with "Bruce Wayne" as Batman's real name. What was the reason for his choice?

- ○ **A.** It was a reference to his favorite comedians Lenny Bruce and Johnny Wayne.
- ○ **B.** It sounded similar to the name of Batman creator Bob Kane.
- ○ **C.** It was a combination of historical figures Robert the Bruce and Mad Anthony Wayne.
- ○ **D.** He had heard the adage "never trust a person with two first names" and thought it fit Batman.

UNSUNG HEROES

Though he created much of the Batman mythos and characters, Bill Finger is still unknown to many. When Bob Kane sold the rights to DC, part of his deal was that he would have a mandatory byline listing him as the creator in all Batman stories and adaptations. Bill Finger's name was never credited. When asked about this, Kane explained that being a ghost writer means not announcing your credit.

18. What former president of DC Comics once described Gotham City as "New York from 14th street down"?

_____

19. In the opening story arc of *JLA: Classified*, an Easter egg implies that Batman once encountered what famous monsters from *Doctor Who*?

_____

20. What famous Batman writer/artist team created Ra's al Ghul?

_____

21. What production designer won an Oscar for designing the Batmobile and the vision of Gotham City in Tim Burton's 1989 film *Batman*?

_____

22. The person from Question 21 also created convincing settings for the film *Full Metal Jacket* in 1987.

○ **A.** True

○ **B.** False

23. Batman's colleague the Elongated Man has been compared to the character Plastic Man, created many years earlier and eventually bought by DC Comics. Why create such a similar hero if DC already had the rights to Plastic Man?

○ **A.** DC Editor Julius Schwartz didn't like Plastic Man and hoped to replace him with a more interesting character.

○ **B.** DC Editor Julius Schwartz was not aware that DC actually had the rights to Plastic Man or else he would have used him.

○ **C.** DC writer Gardner Fox liked Plastic Man's powers and attitude but couldn't take his appearance or name seriously, so he decided to reinvent the character.

○ **D.** Although DC had the rights, the original creator of Plastic Man was suing for royalties and DC did not want to use the character if there was a chance they would lose the court case and have to pay.

24. Along with many Batman stories, writer Mike W. Barr wrote every issue of the first series to star what DC Comics superhero team?

_____

25. What writer created the *Birds of Prey* comic and wrote more than seventy issues of *Nightwing*?

_____

26. Grant Morrison wrote a graphic novel that gave readers the history of Arkham Asylum and remains one of the bestselling graphic novels of all time. It is often called *Batman: Arkham Asylum,* but what is its actual full title?

_____

27. Writer/artist Phil Jimenez wrote a story arc where inmates of Arkham Asylum were inhabited by evil Greek gods. What primary-colored superhero, originally introduced in the 1940s, joined forces with Batman to stop this threat?

_____

28. What was the name of the story arc in Question 27?

_____

29. What popular comic book artist and writer designed the opening title and credits sequence for *Batman Beyond*?

_____

30. In the story "There Is No Hope in Crime Alley!" (1976), writer Dennis O'Neil and artist Dick Giordano created what character who has since become a popular member of Batman's supporting cast?

_____

31. What artist drew the entire Elseworlds trilogy featuring Batman warring against vampires and then becoming one himself?

_____

32. In reference to the graphic novel mentioned in Question 26, Grant Morrison wanted to do something new with the Joker and was told no. What story idea was he not allowed to use?

_____

33. Working together, writer Alan Grant and artist Norm Breyfogle created what two villains who also appeared in the videogame _Batman: Arkham Asylum_?

_____

34. Then-editor Dennis O'Neil supervised _Knightfall, Knight's Quest,_ and _Knight's End_, which featured Batman abandoning his costumed identity due to health reasons, choosing a successor, and then fighting the successor after the latter became unstable. Dennis O'Neil wrote a similar storyline in the 1980s for what Marvel hero who was also a wealthy industrialist like Bruce Wayne?

_____

35. Chuck Dixon wrote the first miniseries to feature Robin as a solo character. Which of the many Robins was the star of this comic?

_____

36. Following the crossover *Zero Hour*, editor Dennis O'Neil decided to change one major aspect of how Batman operated. What was changed?

○ **A.** Batman was now an official deputy of the Gotham City PD.

○ **B.** Batman now operated under a special arrangement with the U.S. government, gaining special resources and access in exchange for sharing what he learned about various criminals and terrorists.

○ **C.** The world believed Batman was dead, allowing him to work clandestinely and convince his enemies that he was an invincible ghost haunting Gotham's streets.

○ **D.** The majority of the world thought Batman an urban myth concocted by the police or the inmates of Arkham Asylum. Those who did believe in him (but had not encountered him) thought the Dark Knight was a supernatural creature.

37. What teenage nephew of a famous spy did Corey Burton play in a cartoon series in 1991?

REMEMBERING THE PAST

Years after Bill Finger's death, artist Jerry Robinson, who had worked on many Batman stories during the early years and helped create the Dark Knight's world, established the Bill Finger Award for Excellence in Comic Writing. This is given annually to two recipients, one living and one deceased, who have not been sufficiently honored in the comic book medium.

58. What American novelist wrote some major stories for Batman and has used the pseudonyms Cliff Garnett and John Harkness?

_____

59. Known for his work portraying the Joker, actor Mark Hamill also played this villain in both the cartoon series *Justice League Unlimited* and the live-action *Flash* TV show. Who is the villain in question?

_____

40. Initially, Batman's symbol was simply a bat silhouette on his shirt. In 1964, Batman changed the symbol to a differently shaped silhouette set against a yellow disc, and it remained this way in his mainstream adventures until what year?

_____

41. When Steve Englehart introduced a new love interest for Batman, what made her stand out from previous ones?

- ○ **A.** She figured out who Batman was on her own, without needing to be told.

- ○ **B.** She was the first woman who obviously had a sexual relationship with Bruce Wayne, whereas Bruce had only casually dated most previous love interests and was never seen kissing them or giving any hint that they spent the night together.

- ○ **C.** She was the first love interest to learn Batman's identity and then not conveniently forget or somehow die.

- ○ **D.** All of the above.

42. During the crossover *Zero Hour*, Dennis O'Neil brought into question whether or not the killer of the Waynes had ever been identified. Why did he do this?

- ○ **A.** He believed it didn't make sense for Batman to continue his crusade if his parents' killer had already met his end somehow.

- ○ **B.** He enjoyed the idea, derived from the films, that the Joker killed Thomas and Martha Wayne; making the murderer unknown created that possibility.

- ○ **C.** He wanted to later reveal that the Waynes were actually killed by the same people who killed Dick Grayson's parents, strengthening the connection between Bruce and Dick.

- ○ **D.** None of the above.

TOO "PSYCHO"?

The 1980s brought a new level of noir to superhero comics. Among the biggest examples were *Watchmen* and *The Dark Knight Returns*, both published in 1986. The latter was penned by Frank Miller, showing an older Batman a decade after he had retired. In the story, Bruce returns to his old role but now has a harsher outlook, regularly hospitalizing criminals with his more violent methods. Miller saw Batman as living on the borderline of becoming just as bad as his enemies. Some later Batman writers imitated this critically acclaimed story less effectively, presenting a Dark Knight who was alarmingly obsessive, dismissive of optimism, and automatically opposed to other superheroes he'd once called friends. Eventually, DC decided this was not the sort of Batman that belonged in the mainstream comics, and the character began to lighten again, especially after the story *Infinite Crisis* when he decided he had lost touch with his original ideals.

43. This writer not only wrote *The Essential Superman Encyclopedia*, he helped put together the series *Who's Who in the DC Universe*. Who is he?

_____

44. What other DC Comics superhero encyclopedia did the writer of Question 43 write?

_____

45. Which Batman writer spent several years of the 1990s regularly putting out seven comic book titles per month?

_____

46. When Dennis O'Neil wrote the story *Batman: Venom*, which takes place in the Dark Knight's past, he intended it to connect to a new villain in the present-day Batman comics.

○ **A.** True

○ **B.** False

47. Which two writers worked together to develop the idea of Hypertime in the 1990s?

_____

48. What was the function of Hypertime?

_____

49. In the late 1990s, Mark Waid and Grant Morrison worked on a proposal to seriously revamp what DC character and make him or her as popular as Batman?

50. Which writer of *He-Man and the Masters of the Universe* later became a major writer, producer, and editor on *Batman: The Animated Series*?

DICK SPRANG

Like Bill Finger, Dick Sprang was not credited for his work in the Batman stories, as his job was that of a ghost artist for Bob Kane. With his cartoonish, simplistic, and vibrant style, he brought a sense of energy and excitement to the Batman comics that meshed wonderfully with Bill Finger's scripts. Together, they had the Dynamic Duo running across the keys of giant typewriters or skittering over the surface of a giant billiard ball.

51. Which two Batman writers made cameos in the episode "Legends of the Dark Mite!" of *Batman: The Brave and the Bold*?

52. Which graphic designer created the covers for *The Complete History of Batman* and *The Golden Age of DC Comics*?

53. The person in Question 52 also worked on a popular book dealing with Batman and Japan. What was its title?

_____

54. Along with Catwoman, what two other characters were featured in Paul Dini's *Gotham Sirens* title?

_____

55. Which one-shot comic, packaged as Bruce Wayne's personal journal, was created as a way for different Batman artists to display their own concepts for a new take on the Batsuit and on Robin's uniform?

_____

56. Which artist of the 1940s created a beloved cover of Batman and Robin in the beam of a searchlight that has constantly been reinterpreted by artists such as Jim Lee and Norm Breyfogle?

_____

57. Which hero in red and green did the artist of Question 56 cocreate with Gardner Fox?

_____

58. When Norm Breyfogle designed the character Anarky, he was deliberately creating a resemblance to what Alan Moore character?

_____

59. Though Bob Kane (and his editor) claimed that the Joker was created in a conversation between him and Bill Finger, which Batman artist consistently insisted the Harlequin of Hate was actually his own creation?

_____

60. What did the artist of Question 59 claim as his inspiration for the Joker?

_____

61. Bob Kane claimed he and Bill Finger got the idea for the Joker primarily from a movie they had seen. What was the film?

_____

62. What actor in the film mentioned in Question 61 bears an eerie resemblance to the original Joker drawings?

_____

63. Working together, Ed Brubaker, Greg Rucka, and Michael Lark created a comic book series that focused on Gotham City cops. What was it called?

_____

64. From the series mentioned in Question 63, Greg Rucka hoped to write a spinoff called _Streets of Gotham_, which would focus on which character?

_____

65. Which supporting cast member of the Superman titles wound up moving to Gotham City and joining the cast of the series mentioned in Question 63?

---

66. Despite critical acclaim and a dedicated fan base, the comic from Question 63 consistently had low sales. When did DC finally decide to cancel it?

- ○ **A.** When a crossover story with Batman failed to improve sales figures.

- ○ **B.** When Greg Rucka was the only one of the three original creators left and he decided it was time to end the run.

- ○ **C.** When new management decided to cut off any titles that didn't feature costumed superheroes.

- ○ **D.** When DC made a decision to cancel the six lowest-selling books, no matter what critical praise they received.

67. In 2005, DC Comics had Dick Grayson propose marriage to Barbara Gordon because the plan was to have him die in the upcoming *Infinite Crisis* crossover.

- ○ **A.** True

- ○ **B.** False

68. Of the different books canceled after *Infinite Crisis*, how many were Batman-related titles?

THE COMICS CODE AUTHORITY

Starting in the 1950s, concerns over comics content caused the industry to impose a rating and censorship system on itself. A stamp on the cover by the Comics Code Authority basically meant this book was safe for kids to read. Initially, the CCA had many rules about content and its presentation. Worst of all for Batman: You could not show how a crime was committed unless impossible methods were involved (superpowers, alien weapons, magic, etc.). *Detective Comics* was now seriously hampered in telling detective stories, leading to strange tales of Batman journeying to other planets or being pestered by magical imps.

69. During DC's famous *Death of Superman* story line, the original plan was to have Batman temporarily relocate to Metropolis so he could take care of the new surge of crime, while Nightwing returned to Gotham and became its primary defender for a while.

- ○ **A.** True
- ○ **B.** False

70. Although Batman and his related characters have maintained a lot of their history in the New 52 continuity, they have been de-aged slightly. Whereas Dick Grayson was in his mid-twenties around the beginning of 2011, how old is he in the new universe?

---

71. After wearing a couple of different costumes with yellow feather designs, Nightwing got what is now considered his "classic" look in the mid-1990s. Which Batman artist designed the black bodysuit with the chevron-style design across the chest?

---

72. In 1948, Bob Kane and Bill Finger created the character of Vicki Vale and designed her to look like which model who later became a famous movie star?

_____

73. When Dennis O'Neil and Neal Adams were designing Ra's al Ghul, they deliberately made his ethnicity vague in order to give him an air of mystery and enhance the atmosphere that this was a man who considered himself beyond the concept of borders and nations.

○ **A.** True

○ **B.** False

74. Dennis O'Neil eventually expressed a desire to cut off Batman's adventures from the rest of the DC Universe because he felt that Batman's presence was not desperately required in a world that had Superman, Green Lantern, Wonder Woman, and other such powerful people who weren't limited to a single city.

○ **A.** True

○ **B.** False

75. According to Dennis O'Neil, there's a rumor that one fan programmed his computer to continually vote for Jason Todd's death, swaying the margin and condemning the teenage hero.

○ **A.** True

○ **B.** False

76. In 1988, DC Comics had the second Robin, Jason Todd, get severely wounded and then wind up in a building with a bomb. After the structure exploded, readers were given the option to vote for Robin's death or his survival by calling one of two hotline numbers. Why did DC choose to do this?

○ **A.** DC Comics was eager to use telephone voting to enhance reader interest, and they chose Robin's life because Dennis O'Neil wasn't sure how to proceed with the not-so-popular character himself.

○ **B.** Originally Wonder Woman's fate was going to be up for voting, but then it was decided to risk Jason Todd's life instead because as a non-powered teenager he would be easy to replace.

○ **C.** Writer Jim Starlin suggested the stunt because Dennis O'Neil wanted to kill the character, on the logic that he wasn't as popular as Dick Grayson. Starlin believed the voting would prove O'Neil wrong and cement Jason Todd's place in the DCU.

○ **D.** DC very much wanted voting on the life or death of a character to generate media attention. Five characters were chosen as candidates, and Jason Todd was then picked at random.

77. In 1980, DC Comics published its second miniseries ever and Batman was the focus. Who wrote it?

_____

78. What was the title of the miniseries in Question 77?

_____

79. The writer mentioned in Question 77 might have been *too* thorough in retelling Batman's origin. The miniseries re-established story concepts that had not been referenced in years and were largely regarded as not being applicable to the more serious, modern-day Batman stories.

○ **A.** True

○ **B.** False

80. What famous Marvel superhero, who was introduced in the pages of *Incredible Hulk* and has been in multiple live-action films, was created by the writer from Question 77?

_____

81. The writer from Question 77 also created what member of Batman's supporting cast who finally made a live-action appearance in *Batman Begins*?

_____

THE NEW LOOK BATMAN

Starting in 1964, Batman was moved in a new direction and his new yellow symbol was part of the package. The authors and artists toned down the campy elements. Rather than dealing with magical transformations or female admirers who attempted to unmask him, the Dark Knight focused on criminal investigation again. Villains were now more dangerous, and some were even tragic figures. The Caped Crusader also began working with other superheroes more often, such as the Justice League of America.

82. This writer of *Batman* and *Batman/Superman* made his screenwriting debut with the movie *Teen Wolf*. Who is he?

_____

83. The writer from Question 82 met DC Comics publisher Jenette Kahn after writing a superhero film script that he failed to sell. What superhero would have starred in this movie?

_____

84. Geoff Johns, as well as the writer from Question 82, and one other writer all share a writing studio called Empathic Magic Tree House. Who is the third writer?

_____

85. The opening story of *Batman: No Man's Land* was written by Bob Gale. He and Rob Zemeckis also wrote which 1980s film starring Michael J. Fox?

_____

86. In 1986, Bob Gale and Robert Zemeckis pitched a Batman film with Michael J. Fox for the role of Robin and Jonathan Frakes as Batman.

○ **A.** True

○ **B.** False

87. When the comic series *Batman: Legends of the Dark Knight* began, there was a rule that lasted for years that while it would feature stories of Batman's early career, Robin was not to appear.

○ **A.** True

○ **B.** False

88. In an issue of *JLA*, which writer intended to include a scene where Batman used a large assault weapon against nonliving enemies but was told no?

_____

89. Which award-winning novelist and comic book writer wrote a two-part story of Batman visiting his own funeral, entitled *Whatever Happened to the Caped Crusader?*

_____

DARKNIGHT DETECTIVE

The 1970s brought Batman and several characters in his world closer to their roots again. During this time, the flashy Batmobiles that looked like futuristic vehicles were replaced by streamlined, turbo-charged roadsters that usually only had a single bat emblem or Batman silhouette on the hood. Batman was drawn more realistically, appearing as a very human athlete in a grounded reality. And his villains again became more lethal.

90. In his Arkham Asylum graphic novel, Grant Morrison decided to accept all the interpretations of the Joker as canon. What about the villain's nature did he propose to explain the Clown Prince of Crime's different styles of behavior over the decades?

○ **A.** Morrison suggested that there is a cult of Jokers, each of whom picks up where the other left off.

○ **B.** Morrison revealed that the Joker is a spirit that shifts from person to person, making them all resemble the same clown but altering his methods slightly in line with their personality.

○ **C.** Morrison had a doctor propose to Batman that the Joker regularly reinvents his identity to adjust to his surroundings and new information he takes in.

○ **D.** Morrison had the Joker hint that he actually had no personality and imitated/exaggerated the qualities of whatever new character or person fascinated him.

Chapter 8 Answer Key

1. D.

2. Neal Adams.

3. *Superman vs. Spider-Man.*

4. Alan Grant.

5. "The Joker's Five-Way Revenge."

6. *L.A. Law.*

7. Grant Morrison.

8. Doug Moench.

9. True.

10. Leonardo da Vinci.

11. Norm Breyfogle.

12. Muhammad Ali.

13. B.

14. The Phantom.

15. True.

16. The Perfesser was Dennis O'Neil and Mastermind was Mike Carlin.

17. C.

18. Paul Levitz.

19. The Daleks.

20. Dennis O'Neil and Neal Adams.

21. Anton Furst.

22. True.

23. B.

24. *Batman and the Outsiders.*

25. Chuck Dixon.

26. *Arkham Asylum: A Serious House on Serious Earth.*

27. Wonder Woman.

28. *Gods of Gotham.*

29. Darwyn Cooke.

30. Leslie Thompkins.

31. Kelley Jones.

32. He wanted to have the Joker cross-dress, symbolizing the character's ever-changing identity and connecting him to the clown fish earlier in the story (clown fish can change gender).

33. Mr. Zsasz and the Ventriloquist.

34. Tony Stark, who turned the identity of Iron Man over to his friend Jim Rhodes when he succumbed to his alcoholism.

35. Tim Drake.

36. D.

37. James Bond Jr.

38. Steve Englehart.

39. The Trickster.

40. 2000.

41. D.

42. A.

43. Robert Greenberger.

44. *The Essential Superman Encyclopedia.*

45. Chuck Dixon.

46. False.

47. Mark Waid and Grant Morrison.

48. It explained away contradictory stories and continuity errors without defining anything as right or wrong.

49. Superman.

50. Paul Dini.

51. Bruce Timm and Paul Dini.

52. Chip Kidd.

53. *Bat-Manga! The Secret History of Batman in Japan.*

54. Poison Ivy and Harley Quinn.

55. *Batman: Knight Gallery.*

56. Jack Burnley.

57. Ted Knight, the first Starman.

58. V from *V for Vendetta*.

59. Jerry Robinson.

60. A playing card with a sinister Joker face on it.

61. *The Man Who Laughs*.

62. Conrad Veidt.

63. *Gotham Central*.

64. Renee Montoya.

65. Maggie Sawyer.

66. B.

67. False.

68. Three.

69. False.

70. 21.

71. Brian Stelfreeze.

72. Marilyn Monroe.

73. True.

74. False.

75. True.

76. A.

77. Len Wein.

78. *The Untold Legend of the Batman*.

79. True.

80. Wolverine.

81. Lucius Fox.

82. Jeph Loeb.

83. The Flash.

84. Allan Heinberg.

85. *Back to the Future*.

86. False (but that would have been *amazing*!)

87. True.

88. Grant Morrison.

89. Neil Gaiman.

90. C.

Score Your Bat-Knowledge!

In this section, there are 90 possible right answers.

If you got 0–40 right, you may know the stories, but you should learn to take a look behind the scenes and find out who brought Batman into being.

If you got 41–65 right, you obviously know some of your favorite writers, but you've still got a lot to learn.

If you got 66–90 right, congratulations! You truly appreciate the creators as much as the stories that entertain you!

CHAPTER 9

BATMAN MISCELLANY

We've covered so much of Batman's reality, but there are still things left to explore. There are the toys. There are bloopers and continuity errors within the films and comics. And then there's the foreign market as well, since Batman has been seen in his own manga series in Japan.

This chapter also throws in last-minute questions and information that may have slipped through the cracks of other chapters. Take a look through and see if you can tackle these bits of trivia as well as you did the others.

1. In the 1989 film *Batman*, Vicki Vale uses a purple mask to protect her from the gas attack that occurs during the Joker's parade. Looking at the mask, why would it have been ineffective?

_____

2. Hopper's Diner appears in the animated film *Batman: Year One*. It was inspired by what famous painting by Edward Hopper?

_____

3. Basil Karlo was the original Clayface in the 1940s and went to prison for his crimes. In 1980, DC Comics reintroduced him in a revised version of the original story. He then wasn't seen in Batman comics again until the 1989 story "Mud Pack" when he came back and sought out his successors, hoping to steal their powers. What's the problem with this?

○ **A.** He made a cameo during the 1986 crossover *Crisis on Infinite Earths*. In the scene, he died alongside Matt Hagen, the second Clayface.

○ **B.** In the 1980 reboot story, it was revealed that Basil Karlo had never been a criminal called Clayface and had actually been murdered by the true villain using that identity.

○ **C.** Basil Karlo was already more powerful than the later beings called "Clayface" and wouldn't have needed to steal their less impressive abilities.

○ **D.** In the 1980 reboot story, Basil Karlo was killed by the Joker soon after he began his career as Clayface.

4. Zsasz appears in *Batman Begins* but the filmmakers misspelled his name. How do they spell it?

_____

5. In the final episode of *Batman: The Brave and the Bold*, Batman used a special piece of mobile equipment that was allegedly inspired by a strange toy product. What was it?

_____

6. The Batmobile from the 1989 film *Batman* has a pair of machine guns that emerge from the hood. The Toy Biz version of this Batmobile replaced the machine guns with a pair of what weapons?

_____

7. In the Batman manga, Lord Death Man is seemingly resurrected. How?

_____

BATMAN THE MANGA

Unlike some heroes, Batman has not been licensed out to a lot of foreign markets. The grim Dark Knight in his gothic urban landscape does not work for some cultures. In Japan, the superhero genre is considered a playground for camp, bright colors, and exaggerated realities. The Batman manga seems less like the creation of Bob Kane and Bill Finger and more like the 1960s Adam West TV show reality with the volume turned up. The manga's writers seem to believe that the absurd must be embraced, and it definitely works for that audience.

8. Continuity alert! How many of these last names have been given for Two-Face's alter ego Harvey?

- ○ **A.** Kent
- ○ **B.** Apollo
- ○ **C.** Dent
- ○ **D.** All of the above

9. In Marvel Comics' *Iron Man*, Tony Stark has an employee named Edwin Jarvis and had an artificial intelligence unit in his main labs named H.O.M.E.R. that built his armors. In the film *Iron Man*, Jarvis was combined with H.O.M.E.R. and was introduced as an A.I. program named J.A.R.V.I.S. This was done because the filmmakers feared that Edwin Jarvis too closely resembled what Batman character?

_____

10. Both Kenner's Super Powers action figure of Robin and Toy Biz's DC Comics Super Heroes action figure of Robin had the same combat move. What was it?

_____

11. The Batman Knight Force Ninja action figures from Kenner sported toys such as Tailwhip Killer Croc and Fist Fury Batman. What was the name of the Riddler's action figure in this toy line?

_____

ADAPTABLE HERO

Batman is a person who has a lot of resources and equipment at hand. Because of this, it's not surprising that he has special suits for special combat situations. Toy companies have taken advantage of this, producing tons of figures in suits that Batman has never worn but that he *might* have worn at some point, given the right circumstances.

12. While pursuing Lord Death Man in the manga series, Batman was seemingly mortally wounded from a gunshot but then recovered, revealing the bullet had only grazed him. How did Batman explain his speedy recovery from what had seemed to be certain death?

○ **A.** "I rejected the bullet through yoga concentration."

○ **B.** "I used force of will to keep the wound from getting serious."

○ **C.** "I'm a Time Lord. We can regenerate. Regeneration's cool."

○ **D.** "I resurrected myself with the strength of righteousness."

13. In the cartoon show *Justice League*, which continued the universe originally set up in *Batman: The Animated Series*, Batman was able to knock out Clayface with a taser. But in Clayface's first story in *Batman:TAS*, what unique feature is he said to have that should've made Batman's attack ineffective?

_____

14. A few of the changes to Batman continuity made by the story *Batman: Year One* were because writer Frank Miller had no real interest in Batman continuity or what changes his new origin might cause.

○ **A.** True

○ **B.** False

15. This Kenner toy based on the film *Batman Returns* featured Batman in a vehicle that could convert to a fighter jet. What was it called?

_____

16. In the film *Batman Begins*, Bruce Wayne is wearing his prototype suit and the memory cloth gloves when he appears in Gordon's office, before he has completed his Batman suit. What small continuity error is present here?

_____

17. In the Batman manga series, what club was the ideal place where Gotham's rich gentlemen could relax and socialize?

_____

18. In an episode of the 1960s live-action Batman show, Alfred once accidentally called Dick Grayson (played by Burt Ward) . . .

○ **A.** Master Burt

○ **B.** Master Bird

○ **C.** Mister Ward

○ **D.** Master Mister

19. One of the DC Direct Black and White statues of Batman was designed by comic artist Cliff Chiang. This statue features Batman wielding what weapons that aren't normally associated with him?

_____

20. In 1991, Kenner made a *Batman Returns* toy featuring Robin mounted on a "Jet Foil Cycle" that could fire ground-level missiles—despite the fact that he didn't appear in the film.

○ **A.** True

○ **B.** False

21. The Collector's Edition of the videogame *Batman: Arkham Asylum* comes with a journal concerning the Arkham inmates, a code for a downloadable challenge map, a behind-the-scenes DVD, and a fourteen-inch model of what weapon?

_____

22. Which criminal did *not* appear in *Batman: The Lazarus Syndrome*?

○ **A.** The Joker

○ **B.** Talia al Ghul

○ **C.** Black Mask

○ **D.** Ra's al Ghul

23. In Batman's Japanese comic adventures, he fought Go-Go the Magician. Go-Go's powers and suit seemed to emulate what popular Flash villain?

_____

24. *Batman: The Lazarus Syndrome* takes place soon after the death of Jason Todd and references the event.

○ **A.** True

○ **B.** False

NINJA ACTION FIGURES

Another thing that allows toy companies to milk Batman for more figures is the fact that he is essentially a ninja. Since ninjas often have waves of popularity in the action/adventure genre, this means you can do entire new figures that dress up Batman and his allies based on different ideas of what weapons a ninja may use and style or body armor they may wear.

25. Adam Beane sculpted the Batman: The Dark Crusader mini-statue based on a painting by what famous comic book artist?

_____

26. Originally, the baby featured in *Batman: Year One* was intended by writer Frank Miller to be Babs Gordon, who would grow up to become Batgirl.

○ **A.** True

○ **B.** False

27. According to *Batman: The Lazarus Syndrome*, what unusual law exists in Gotham City?

○ **A.** It is illegal to operate as a masked vigilante without approval from Commissioner Gordon and Batman.

○ **B.** It is illegal to claim to be an agent of Batman's without a badge identifying you as a member of Batman, Inc.

○ **C.** Assaulting Batman and his forces is considered the same as assaulting a police officer.

○ **D.** It is illegal to impersonate Batman.

28. Mattel's *Batman Legacy* figure of the Golden Age Joker features the character wielding what weapon?

_____

29. In the film *The Dark Knight*, Bruce plans to fly into Hong Kong by having a pilot fly under the radar and then H.A.L.O. jumping to the ground. Based on what H.A.L.O. stands for, why does this not quite make sense?

_____

30. The Batman Knight Force Ninja figure called Fist Fury Batman displayed the Dark Knight in a new costume. What was the strange choice for its dominant color?

_____

31. Who was the villain Karmak in Batman's manga adventures?

   ○ **A.** A telepathic dragon.

   ○ **B.** A superpowered, intelligent gorilla in a mask.

   ○ **C.** An alien with shadow powers.

   ○ **D.** A superpowered, intelligent wolf-man in a mask.

32. According to Alfred in *Batman: The Lazarus Syndrome*, how many Batmobiles are held in the Batcave?

_____

33. The Legends of the Batman action figure Power Guardian Batman showed a version of the Dark Knight who wore a collared cape, thigh-high boots, a shield, and what kind of sword?

_____

34. Despite the fact that Robin has had a number of personalized vehicles over the years, none of them have been made into toys for children.

○ **A.** True

○ **B.** False

35. In _Batman Returns_, what happens to Catwoman's high heels when she's doing her backflips?

_____

36. When his origin was later revealed, it was said that the man called Mr. Zsasz had once been the wealthy head of his own international company before later becoming a killer. But in his very first appearance, Zsasz said (and demonstrated, through his clothing choice) that his previous career had been . . . what?

_____

37. In *Detective Comics* #328, Batman was seen drawing a gun from his belt despite his earlier repeated vows not to use one. What explains this out-of-character weapon?

○ **A.** He was under hypnosis and acting on the orders of a criminal.

○ **B.** It was actually a nonlethal weapon, but Batman needed to scare the criminals he was confronting by convincing them he'd become a killer.

○ **C.** DC Editor Julius Schwartz was unaware that Batman did not use firearms.

○ **D.** Batman had intended to draw a grappling hook launcher but the Joker had switched this device with a gun in order to frame the hero for a murder he'd committed.

38. In *Batman Returns*, the penguin exhibit in Gotham's zoo is called Arctic World. Why is this wrong?

_____

39. In *Batman Begins*, the Gotham City Police Department cars have the initials "GPD" stenciled on them. But what do the police officers have stenciled on their jackets instead?

_____

40. Kenner's Legends of Batman toy line produced a figure called Crusader Robin. This featured Robin wearing medieval armor, a bat-shield, a helmet, and what weapon?

_____

41. Mattel's Martial Arts Batman action figure featured the Dark Knight wearing what strange new item of clothing?

○ **A.** A bandana with a bat symbol

○ **B.** A kendo helmet with bat ears

○ **C.** A yin yang belt buckle

○ **D.** A sash decorated by bat symbols

42. In the Batman manga series, Dr. Denton seemed to be a criminal, but this was a ruse. What was the name of the villain who was masquerading as Dr. Denton?

_____

43. Kenner's Legends of Batman toy line produced an action figure of Jean Paul Valley, depicting when he assumed the role of Batman and wearing gold-and-blue armor. What did they call this figure?

_____

44. In the beginning of the story *Final Crisis*, Batman examined the body of the heroic New God called Orion. Batman found that Orion had been killed by a time-traveling bullet. But before *Final Crisis* was released, what miniseries had shown Orion being killed by an explosion?

_____

45. Who was the current Robin during the story *Batman: The Lazarus Syndrome*?

○ **A.** There was no active Robin in the story.

○ **B.** Jason Todd

○ **C.** Tim Drake

○ **D.** Carrie Kelley

46. In between the publication of *Final Crisis* and the depiction of his explosive death a few months earlier, Orion appeared in the final issues of the series *Countdown*, determined to kill his father Darkseid. How did the final issue of the story mentioned in Question 44 explain the seeming mistake of Orion's appearance in *Countdown*?

_____

47. For its Legends of the Batman toy line, Kenner made a figure that seemed to combine Batman with Robin Hood. What was it called?

_____

48. The Super Power Collection action figure of Batman advertised a combat move. What was it called?

○ **A.** Bat-Punch

○ **B.** Power Action Bat Punch

○ **C.** Action Kick

○ **D.** Super Action Karate Chop

49. What toy based on the 1989 film *Batman* could be bought with a plastic cocoon?

_____

50. The action figure of "Bob, the Joker's Goon" from the 1989 *Batman* film had what special feature when you pressed a button?

- ○ **A.** Judo Punch
- ○ **B.** Kung-Fu Kick
- ○ **C.** Power Kick
- ○ **D.** Spinning Punch

51. Years before Christopher Nolan directed *Batman Begins*, director Darren Aronofsky was said to be attached to a live-action adaptation of *Batman: Year One*.

- ○ **A.** True
- ○ **B.** False

52. What was the name of the action figure from the Legends of the Dark Knight toy line that featured Robin with a battle staff; a utility gauntlet; and a camouflage cape of light blue, dark blue, and electric purple?

- ○ **A.** Battle Gear Robin
- ○ **B.** Super Action Robin
- ○ **C.** Ground Assault Robin
- ○ **D.** Jungle Rage Robin

53. In an episode of *Batman: The Brave and the Bold* entitled "Night of the Batmen!" the Dark Knight awakens in an infirmary and sees the Martian Manhunter nearby, standing beside several burning candles. Why should the Martian Manhunter not be so calm at this moment?

ELSEWORLDS AS TOYS

The Legends of the Batman toy line seems to have been inspired by Elseworlds comics. Each toy put Batman and Robin into a different setting that would be unusual for their mainstream comic book adventures. Likewise, the figures were altered to fit in with the settings, wearing chain mail for medieval environments and so on.

54. Mattel's DC Universe Classic Series toy line features a version of Batman dressed as a member of what intergalactic group with powers based on the emotion of fear?

55. The Batman Knight Force Ninja toy called Arsenal Cape Batman featured the Dark Knight wearing a version of his costume that used a different color scheme. What was it?

- ○ **A.** Red and Blue
- ○ **B.** Purple and Green
- ○ **C.** Purple and Orange
- ○ **D.** Red and White

56. According to *Batman: The Lazarus Syndrome*, Dick Grayson's nickname as a child (beyond "Boy Wonder") was what?

_____

57. In *The Dark Knight* (2008), Lucius Fox has a meeting in Hong Kong. From the terrace, you can see the McCormick Place buildings in the background. What city is the actual location of those buildings?

_____

58. Tonner dolls made figures of all but one of these characters. Which one?

○ **A.** Poison Ivy

○ **B.** Oracle

○ **C.** Harley Quinn

○ **D.** Batgirl

59. In the Total Justice toy line, various superheroes wore a new type of armor that worked with their natural abilities. What was the armor called?

_____

60. In *The Dark Knight* (2008), Two-Face speaks to Gordon via his cell phone and then hangs up, leaving Gordon with a dial tone for a moment before he goes into action. What is wrong with this scene?

_____

61. Kenner Toys released a comic with the Cyber-Link Superman and Batman Action Figure Two-Pack. What was the title of the comic?

○ **A.** *Superman & Batman: Cyber Warriors*

○ **B.** *Superman & Batman: Cyber Doom*

○ **C.** *Superman & Batman: Linked Destinies*

○ **D.** *Superman & Batman: Doom Link*

62. SkyDive Batman featured the Dark Knight in what color?

_____

63. Figures of Harley Quinn from *Batman: Arkham City* were pulled from the shelves of Midtown Comics in New York City due to complaints of lewdness.

○ **A.** True

○ **B.** False

64. Mattel released *Batman: The Brave and the Bold* Transforming Batmobile. What does this car transform into?

_____

65. In the Super Friends action figure lines, what kind of vehicle was the Joker usually seen driving?

_____

66. Batman and Robin were once used to advertise candy cigarettes.

○ **A.** True

○ **B.** False

67. In the 1980s, Batman PJs for kids came with capes that could attach to the shoulders with Velcro.

○ **A.** True

○ **B.** False

68. Aside from an actual utility belt, what noticeable item of Batman's costume was not included with the PJs from Question 67?

_____

69. Harley Quinn dresses as a nurse in *Batman: Arkham Asylum*. Some fans took issue with this because it did not accurately reflect her original profession. How so?

_____

CONTINUITY

Despite the fact that DC Comics occasionally reboots its universe, continuity errors seem unavoidable. Batman has many monthly titles; when you combine that with his guest appearances in other books, the fact that he's often involved in the Justice League, and the titles that involve Robin, Batwoman, or any of the Batgirls, you realize that this is a large group of writers and editors to coordinate.

70. A plush toy of Scarecrow was sold by Mattel; thanks to refillable "fear gas" cartridges it could spray smoke.

○ **A.** True

○ **B.** False

71. The Batman Manga comics featured Lord Death Man. In what American comic book did Lord Death Man make his U.S. debut?

_____

72. What Japanese hero did Batman seek out in the comic mentioned in Question 71?

_____

Chapter 9 Answer Key

1. The mask has no filters on it.
2. Nighthawks.
3. B.
4. Zsaz.
5. Neon Talking Super-Street Bat-Luge.
6. Missiles.
7. He used yoga tricks to simulate death.
8. D.
9. Alfred.
10. Karate chop.
11. Tornado Blade Riddler.
12. D.
13. Clayface was not affected by electricity.
14. True.
15. Batblade.
16. He hadn't gotten memory cloth yet.
17. The Parro Club.
18. A.
19. Guns.
20. True.
21. Batarang.
22. C.
23. Weather Wizard.
24. True.
25. Alex Ross.
26. True.
27. D.
28. A sledgehammer.
29. H.A.L.O. is High Altitude–Low Opening, which means Bruce would not have been *under* the radar.
30. Neon Green.
31. B.
32. Six.
33. Fencing saber.
34. False.
35. They temporarily become flats.
36. Magician.
37. C.
38. Penguins live in Antarctica, not the Arctic.
39. GCPD.
40. Crossbow.
41. D.
42. Morgan.
43. KnightsEnd Batman.
44. *Death of the New Gods*.
45. A.
46. The last issue of *Death of the New Gods* showed Orion's ghost being called forth by the Source so he could fight Darkseid again. Of course, being able to fight his father meant he would need physical form again, so in essence this became a full-blown resurrection.
47. Crusader.
48. B.
49. The Batmobile.
50. A.
51. True.
52. D.
53. He has pyrophobia.
54. Sinestro Corps.
55. C.
56. The Robin Hood of the Flying Trapeze.
57. Chicago.
58. B.
59. Fractal.

60. Cell phones don't have dial tones.

61. D.

62. Orange.

63. False.

64. A jet.

65. A van.

66. True.

67. True.

68. A mask.

69. She was a doctor, not a nurse.

70. False.

71. *Batman Incorporated* #1.

72. Mr. Unknown.

Score Your Bat-Knowledge!

In this section, there are 72 possible right answers.

If you got 0–32 right, you need to expand your trivia horizons.

If you got 33–54 right, you've done pretty well, but you're not a Dark Knight yet.

If you got 55–72 right, congratulations! You truly have a superb knowledge of Batman's toys, bloopers, and foreign interpretations!

FAN SCORECARD

Now it's time to see if you've got the all-around chops to call yourself a true fan of Batman! Flip back to the end of each answer key to find your chapter scores and write them down here for easy reference. Then add them up and see where you stand on the Fan Spectrum.

_____ **CHAPTER 1** (145 possible points)

_____ **CHAPTER 2** (72 possible points)

_____ **CHAPTER 3** (67 possible points)

_____ **CHAPTER 4** (128 possible points)

_____ **CHAPTER 5** (52 possible points)

_____ **CHAPTER 6** (140 possible points)

_____ **CHAPTER 7** (82 possible points)

_____ **CHAPTER 8** (90 possible points)

_____ **CHAPTER 9** (72 possible points)

_____ **TOTAL** (848 possible points)

IF YOU . . .

- scored 763 to 848, you're an **EXPERT!** If you could compare your scores to Bruce Wayne, you might finally penetrate behind that forbidding mask! Be gentle with the egos of everyone below you—they have much to learn from your ultimate Bat-sense!

- scored 678 to 762, you're a **CONNOISSEUR!** When it comes to Batman, you've got it down. You could make educated guesses about where the franchise might go because you know just about everywhere it's been!

- scored 594 to 677, you're a **TRUE FAN!** You've got far more than just "the basics" down about your favorite Caped Crusader, and you probably have very few friends who doubt your bat-knowledge. A little brushing up, and you'll be an Expert in no time!

- scored 508 to 593, you're a **BUFF!** Your utility belt must be fully stocked—because you're off to a great start! You've got most people beat when it comes to knowing what there is to know about the Dark Knight!

- scored less than 508, you're an **ENTHUSIAST!** You might have some studying to do to boost your bat-smarts, but that just means there are more comics, movies, video-games, and radio plays in your future!

INDEX

Note: Page numbers in *italics* indicate Answer Key answers.

About the Author

Alan Kistler is an actor and writer who co-hosts the weekly podcast *Crazy Sexy Geeks*. Along with contributing articles to various websites, he writes the "Agent of S.T.Y.L.E." weekly column on Newsarama.com and is also the author of *The Unofficial Game of Thrones Cookbook*. A pop culture historian focusing on comic books and sci-fi/fantasy, Alan has been featured by CNN, MTV, Epix, the *New York Daily News*, Warner Bros. Home Video, and NPR Radio 360. He lives in New York, New York.